Methodist Spiritua

Exploring Methodism

Methodist Spirituality

Gordon S. Wakefield

EPWORTH PRESS

0 7162 0525 4

First published 1999
by Epworth Press
20 Ivatt Way
Peterborough, PE3 7PG

Typeset by Rowland Phototypesetting Limited
Bury St Edmunds, Suffolk
and printed in Great Britain by
Redwood Books, Trowbridge, Wilts

In Grateful Memory

CHARLES HERBERT BROWN M.A.
(1882–1965)

ERNEST WARNER
(1888–1960)

Methodist Ministers

Contents

Preface to the Series

What is Methodism and how did it begin? What did John Wesley teach? We sing Charles Wesley's hymns but what can we discover about his life? What is the character and work of the Methodist Church today? What have Methodists had to say about social issues? What place have women had in Methodism? These are the kind of questions which *Exploring Methodism* is aiming to answer.

All of the contributors are experts in their field, and all write in an attractive way that will appeal to both church members and everyone interested in the life and history of the churches. The format of the books enables each writer to introduce extracts from the writings of the main characters and official church documents, and in this way to bring the reader close to what was actually said and written by the leaders of the church and church members. It is hoped that the books will be studied in house groups and other discussion groups as well as read by individuals, and questions for discussion, directly related to the present day, are included at the end of each chapter. Each volume contains an annotated list of books for further reading.

Barrie Tabraham opened the series with a general overview of Methodist history. He was followed by John Munsey Turner who traced the life and thinking of the Methodist Church from 1932 to the present day and then by Thomas Langford, who explored the development of Methodist theology. In the present volume, Gordon Wakefield uses his wide experience and understanding of the spiritual influences which have fed Methodism to set Methodist piety and devotion in its wider setting. Forthcoming volumes will cover the life and work of Charles Wesley, music in Methodism, official statements by the Church on social and political issues, the activity of women in early Methodism, Methodist preachers and preaching, and other topics.

Cyril S. Rodd

Foreword

Methodism is a coat of many colours. Though its roots may be found mainly in Puritan and Anglican soil, it is indebted to a variety of other Christian traditions – Lutheran, Moravian, Roman Catholic and Orthodox. No one is more sensitively aware of this varied texture of Methodism, in theology and spirituality, than Dr Gordon Wakefield. As the Editor of a standard *Dictionary of Christian Spirituality*, he is able to set Methodist piety and devotion in its wider setting, as well as bringing out its particular quality and identity.

The variety of spiritual influences which have fed Methodism is reflected in the diversity of devotional practice among the Methodist people. Gordon Wakefield stands in the High Wesleyan tradition, but his genuinely catholic spirit enables him to enter with insight and appreciation into other strands of Methodist piety, whether Bible Christian, Primitive Methodist, or Charismatic.

The result is a splendid introduction to Methodist spirituality, which is enlivened by Dr Wakefield's willingness to draw on his own personal faith and family reminiscences in lighting up his subject. His book is not only a sure guide to the history of Methodist spirituality, it also addresses current needs and contemporary discipleship. Moreover, it is the work of one who not only writes of Methodist spirituality, but lives it.

John A. Newton

Author's Preface

In 1966, I was invited to give the Wesley Historical Society lecture at the Wolverhampton Conference. It was published as a short book, *Methodist Devotion: The Spiritual Life in the Methodist Tradition 1791–1945*. It has been suggested that I revise and in parts re-write this for the 'Exploring Methodism' series.

Since 1966, there has been much writing on 'spirituality' and, both here and in the States, on Methodism. There have also been great changes both in the Christian churches and in Methodism. This book seeks to carry the story to the present day. It pillages much of what I have written on Wesley and Methodism over the years, notably my life of Robert Newton Flew. Other of my pieces will be acknowledged in the notes. It is very much indebted to the three volumes of *A History of the Methodist Church in Great Britain*, edited by Rupert E. Davies, A. Raymond George and E. Gordon Rupp, and to various writings of the Revd John Munsey Turner, notably his Fernley-Hartley lecture of 1982, *Conflict and Reconciliation*. I must repeat my gratitude to the late Revd A. Raymond George for his paper on *Private Devotion in the Methodist Tradition* printed in *Studia Liturgica* Volume II, Number 3, September 1963. Above all, I have used the so far unpublished PhD thesis of the Revd Dr Ian Randall, Church History Tutor at Spurgeon's College, London, for the sections on the Holiness Movement of the twentieth century and the Fellowship of the Kingdom. I am most grateful for his generous permission. The previous book did not deal adequately with Cliff College and the preaching of entire sanctification.

My debt to my wife for her help in preparation for the press and for her unfailing patience as I remove myself to the study, and to Margaret Lydamore of SCM Press, is incalculable.

The section on the nineteenth century is the least altered from 1966.

The book cites many publications, but fundamental is personal memory and experience. Thanks to my mother's reminiscences and my cradle Methodism, I have in effect lived through developments since 1880. I repeat the account of my maternal grandfather's addresses to his society class. I have also had in my possession since 1992 the very different literary remains of T. S. Gregory, 'a saint and near genius', according to Gordon Rupp, who became a Roman Catholic in 1935. I have had to fight him becoming a digression.

The book is part of the story of my life and ministry which, as it has turned out, has been much concerned with spirituality. I was Chairman of the President's Commission in 1973–74, as well as Editor of the SCM Press *Dictionary of Christian Spirituality* in 1983. The writing of the following pages and the encounters involved have been for me a devotional exercise, bringing me nearer to the Divine presence, especially as I have read the inter-war Manuals of Fellowship and been aware once more of Maltby, Flew and Findlay. I write as a traditional Wesleyan with ecumenical predispositions. I grieve that 'our hymns' do not seem to be sung and prayed over as they were at my beginnings. I believe that perfect love is the goal of the Christian life, in spite of the abuses of perfectionism. I would hope that though the book may not rehabilitate the hymns, it may, in the words of one of the greatest still much sung, not least in the Church of England, confirm our hearts desire 'to work and speak and think for thee'.

Gordon S. Wakefield

Introduction

Spirituality is a term much in vogue. There are various accounts of its history and uses, but today it refers to those disciplines and practices which are to assist in the fulfilment of what is believed to be the purpose of human life. This enters a realm beyond mere survival and bodily needs. For the Nazis this was the dominance of the Aryan races. For Marxists it is the abolition of capitalism and the creation, by strict controls, of a society of equals, in which labour has true value. For Christians it is growth in grace, that is in the goodness and love which are both the nature and the gift of God himself; Christlikeness puts it in a word; the kingdom or rule of God is its social consequence. This is achieved through the possession of the Holy Spirit which Christ bestowed on his disciples as a result of his passion. The Spirit was released by his self-giving on the cross and his resurrection, which made available his own eternal life to those who trusted in him.

I do not think that any Christians would disagree with that. But there are differences and distinctions as to whether, say, spirituality is imposed by church authority, or is an individual's or group's conclusions from faith in God's act in Christ. The one may arise out of the other. Dogma may be formulated spirituality.

Other factors are involved: geography, for instance. Why is the spirituality of Northern Europe different from that of the Mediterranean countries; or Eastern Christianity from Western; or Celtic from Roman? Why did the mystical movement of fourteenth-century England originate in the East Midlands and East Anglia?

In considering Methodist spirituality, social context is very important. Methodism arose because of the personal experiences of John and Charles Wesley, the influences that shaped them, the home in which they were reared, the books they read, the people they met. Methodism was not the whole of the evangelical revival and Methodists have tended to exaggerate its triumphs, but it was right for the time. It reached the unchurched populations of the newly industrialized England, the victims of unrelenting penal laws, and those who would advance from social ostracism and insecurity to 'decent' poverty and respectability, who were to become the lower middle class, always striving for advance, educationally and socially, if not spiritually. It was found in the grocer's shop and, not least, among the miners, whose harsh and hazardous lives were given meaning by Methodism, rather than relieved and often ruined by strong drink. It helped their advance by law-abiding means.

After Wesley's death and for the first half of the nineteenth century, there were political tensions within Methodism. Jabez Bunting, the Wesleyan leader, said 'Methodism hates democracy as it hates sin'. Other Methodists separated amid bitter controversy in the interests of more democratic church government. Methodists took different views in the reactionary aftermath of the Napoleonic wars and the mid-century continental revolutions and the birth of nation states. What is often ignored in discussions of spirituality is that in the hundred years between 1767 when the Wesleys were in full flow, and the publication of Marx's *Das Capital*, 'the face of England had completely altered; social life had been transformed from top to bottom, the spirit and temper of society had been profoundly changed' . There was a more obvious transformation in men's ways of life, their ordinary everyday wants and expectations, in this period than there had been for hundreds of years before. 'Can anyone maintain that the Industrial Revolution was not the predominant cause in that transformation?'[1]

Later, with the nonconformist bodies, Methodism became one of the Free Churches, predominantly Liberal in politics and destined to decline with the Liberal Party, though some Methodists were Socialists and prominent in the Trade Unions and the Labour Party. Did they share a common spirituality? They all sang Wesley hymns, though the Prayer Book tradition of Wesley was represented in a tenacious minority of Wesleyans. The sacramental tradition was lost as Anglo-Catholicism exerted its increasing and immense, though in the end temporary dominance, and Rome seemed menacingly to loom. In church architecture the Gothic revival prevailed in many places over the preaching auditorium. This was true among Congregationalists and Unitarians as well. In some places this was due to a desire to out-steeple the Church of England. The spire of Trinity Methodist Church, Abingdon-on-Thames, had to be higher than that of St Helen's Parish Church. Methodist identity and strength needed to be conspicuous and socially prominent. Music became the dominant art-form with oratorios much sung in chapels and, later, concerts of light opera on church premises, which provided for social as well as religious and educational activities.

The Methodist virtues of temperance and thrift, of honesty and plain dealing led to prosperity, just as they did to education. In the 1790s there was in Derbyshire an illiterate Wesleyan who taught himself to read from a tombstone in Hathersage churchyard. By the 1870s his descendant had secured a first-class degree at Oxford. By the end of the century, Methodist biblical scholarship was influential in both ancient universities. W. F. Moulton, Headmaster of the Leys School at Cambridge – a Wesleyan public school – was a colleague of the great Anglican trio, Lightfoot, Westcott and Hort and one of the revisers of the English Bible. His son, James Hope, was the first non-Anglican Fellow of King's College, who went on to become a Professor at Manchester, as did the Primitive Methodist layman, A. S. Peake of Merton College, Oxford. Peake gave his name to a famed one-volume commentary on the Bible. There is little trace of academic snobbery. Both Moulton and Peake were committed to Methodism's evangelical mission and were very much one in fellowship with the ministers and lay people. Peake helped to produce a Primitive Methodist ministry competent in the biblical languages; and Lincolnshire ploughboys would rise in the small hours to study Greek in preparation for ministerial training. But there were controversies over the higher criticism and some battles to be fought. The fundamentalist Wesley Bible Union caused church leaders and scholars some troubles during the 1914 war, while at least one Methodist woman in Devon thanked God at the news of Peake's death in 1929. The enlightened felt that criticism could wonderfully illuminate the scriptures. They spoke confidently until the 1950s or 60s, of 'assured results', which while disproving inerrancy had established the sovereign truth of the Bible. Such confidence has now been lost, as we realize how little we really know for certain of Christian origins, while we are more aware of unscriptural interpretations of Christ, such as the Gospel of Thomas with its lack of a passion story, the Dead Sea Scrolls, the sacred texts of other religions and the perennial tendency of Christians to bend the Bible to their own ideological and social presuppositions. Biblical scholars are hypersensitive to sexism in scripture and the promotion of antisemitism in the New Testament. James Hope Moulton always reverentially lowered his voice when he named Jesus Christ in lectures. Some very old-fashioned Roman Catholic priests may do so still, or raise their birettas at the sacred name, but in the world of scholarship this is not likely to happen. Professor Moule may have been the last to open his lectures in the Cambridge Divinity Faculty with prayer.

Meanwhile there is the phenomenon called post-modernism. This disregards and is sceptical towards the great stories which Christianity, and Marxism, for instance, offer as the interpretations of the human condition. Tradition is useless and its transmission through education void. Post-modernism is inimical to the attempt to discover the author's meaning in a passage. The reader is paramount, which makes the quest for objective truth impossible and could reinforce fundamentalism, which has sprung up in all major religions.

There was a division between those who saw Methodists as a church with its own understanding of the church's nature, finely presented and approved by the Conference of the United Church in a report of 1937, and those who thought of Methodism principally as a movement for the revival of evangelical Christianity in the national life. This last demanded freedom of worship, the extempore – an important part of the Wesley heritage – rather than the liturgical. The former now suffers because the historical record of Christian institutions is seen as so mixed. Far less than Christ, whose message many believe was perverted by it, the church is no longer spoken of in triumphalist tones. Even if it has not misunderstood Jesus, it cannot be claimed to be the source of all good in human life. The Enlightenment, now regarded by some Christians as an enemy, has been responsible for many of the humane benefits and scientific advances which we enjoy. Evangelicalism has to contend with prevailing secularization, a culture which ignores Christianity, as that of Wesley's day certainly did not. The gospel is no longer seen as relevant to the realities of life and the universe as we know them, while there is an emergence of new religious movements outside the major historic faiths. We live in a free market, for religion as everything else. Post-modern society has been called a 'pleasure-dome'. Entertainment and publicity are the great industries, together with tourism and catering – 'Methodism and the miner' means nothing any more in Western society – and the making of money, indeed the worship of mammon, is the great goal of human endeavour, for which traditional moral values may be forfeit. And God's power is superseded by the human ability to do all things, to govern by computer, to clone life and, of course, to destroy the planet. In spirituality Methodists have ceased to be distinctive. There has been a great increase in evangelicalism, which has sidelined Wesley. 'Our hymns' are considered too verbose in an age of soundbite religion and repeated mantras rather than theological depth, while modern translations obscure their biblical references. Music too has changed, so that congregational singing is no longer the inspiration it was. Other Methodists turn to Catholic forms of spirituality. There is a retreat group and many have been influenced by the spirituality of Ignatius Loyola, founder of the Jesuits, and his Spiritual Exercises. These, as interpreted by such as Father Gerard Hughes, have proved to be remarkably flexible, adaptable and interdenominational. John Wesley, who was not without admiration for Ignatius and recommended meditation, would not have disapproved, much as he shared, in spite of his Dublin letter to a Roman Catholic in 1749, the anti-Roman prejudices of Hanoverian England.

Mysticism has perennial attraction. It is not tied to history which may be vulnerable to research, increased knowledge and conflicting interpretations, or to tradition, since its quest is for an immediacy of union with God. And it may unite religions, as Aldous Huxley tried to show years ago in *The Perennial Philosophy*.

A friend of mine spent some time in the spring of 1997 at the bedside of Mother Teresa in Calcutta. Aged and weak she kept repeating 'Pray for peace' and 'Remember the poor'. There is evidence that these counsels are making possible a revival of an ecumenical spirituality of social action, though some Christians are chary of any direct involvement of the churches in politics and believe that spirituality transcends political divisions and should concern itself with realities not of this world.

From the 1890s to the 1960s Methodism was much influenced by the Temperance Movement, and the Methodist was regarded by virtue of the fact as a teetotaller, often to the gentle teasing of friends in other denominations. That has much changed due to the fact that alcohol is inescapable in our culture and drink enters every living room through television. In R. Newton Flew's much reprinted manual of the early 1920s on *The Forgiveness of Sins* there is quoted a letter about a friend who had let in his son one midnight and found him drunk. 'It seemed to him as if his home had fallen in ruins about him that night.' Though the evils of alcoholism are more than ever apparent, it is not now clear that a modern Methodist would find such an incident so devastating and such a test of forgiveness.

Professor Richard H. Rogers has wondered if there might not be a 'Balkan' aspect to the spiritual problems of the post-modern period. He cites an example from Scotland and William Scorrar's book, *Christian Identity: A Scottish Approach*. In spite of one-worldism and moves towards European unity, nationalism may be undergoing a revival. In Scotland this might result in a new consciousness of what has been distinctive in the past and a re-functioning of Celtic spirituality, with its awareness of nature, amid modern technology. England is more multinational and cultural since the 1950s. Is the revival of an English spirituality, so much that of the now largely discarded *Book of Common Prayer*, a possibility? Rogers thinks that in this 'solution' there might be an evasion of the criticism of the past.

He believes that we need to mobilize all Christian resources, the total inheritance. 'The Tradition as a whole in its variety offers enormous resources, symbolic, mythic, narrative, ethical, theological.' These must be assembled and brought to bear in a scrutiny of the human condition.[2]

'To serve the present age', a traditional Methodist vocation, should be the watchword. In this there could be a contribution from traditional Methodist spirituality, the history and developments of which are the subject of this book. It will need to be as ecumenical as Wesley in its search for resources and even learn from other faiths. Its distinctive contribution may be an ethos of warmth and friendship, together with what Alexander Knox described as 'that cheerful piety, habitual pleasure in devotion and consequent settled self-enjoyment, which John Wesley maintained to be the inheritance of the true Christian'.[3]

PART I

WESLEY'S LEGACY

I

Before 1738

Early influences on Wesley

John Wesley is not reliable on dates and is apt to give differing versions of his spiritual biography, but in this statement [1], he sees the origins of Methodism at the time he returned to Oxford as a Fellow of Lincoln College from a period as his father's curate at Wroot. His brother Charles was at Christ Church and had turned to spiritual seriousness. They belonged to what was sneeringly called the 'Holy Club' or the 'Methodists', a loosely-knit group of students and dons who had met to help each other with their studies but also, increasingly, to deepen their spiritual lives. They did this by rule of life, regular observance of the offices and the sacraments of the church and works of philanthropy, such as visiting prisoners and showing charity to the poor. The group was rather accident prone. Some of its members overdid the austerities. One, William Morgan, died insane.

Another had a nervous breakdown. He was the son of the landlord of the Bell Inn at Gloucester, and a servitor at Pembroke College, one who earned his keep and academic instruction by waiting on the wealthier students and performing menial college tasks. He recovered through reading a book lent him by Charles Wesley, *The Life of God in the Soul of Man*, by the Scottish Episcopalian Henry Scougal. His name was George Whitefield and he became the greatest popular preacher since Hugh Latimer and began the Evangelical Revival, in 1737.

By 1729 John Wesley had been a serious Christian for some years. He had read widely, not least in secular literature, including *Gulliver's Travels*, Shakespeare and, to the shock of later Methodists, Restoration Comedy. Oxford would ground him in the early fathers of the church, the Greek and Latin theologians of the years before the Council of Nicaea in 325. He regarded a knowledge of them as among the chief privileges of a university education. He was not blind to their faults and weaknesses. In a letter to Dr Conyers Middleton, he compared them to some of his own Methodists, post-Oxford. They were not gifted with great learning, at times they argued their case badly, but 'they were Christians' and their writings 'describe true, genuine Christianity'. He was, as always, catholic in his spiritual reading in that he was not inhibited by confessional barriers. He read Edward Sheldon's translation of the life of Gaston Jean Baptiste de Renty (1611–1649) by Saith-Jure. He began preparing a synopsis of it in 1729, though he did not publish an abridged version until 1741. De Renty was a Parisian nobleman who was married, though seems to have learned a holy detachment from his wife as well as from his wealth. He founded a society of ladies for what was virtually the perpetual adoration of the Blessed Sacrament. He combined mysticism with philanthropy in a remarkable way. He was at once intensely dedicated, writing out a covenant with Christ in his own blood, penetrating by contemplation into the mysteries of the Holy Trinity, and yet caring for the sick, the aged, the exiled and gathering around him groups of Christians whom Henry Bett regarded as the true precursors of the Methodist class-meeting.[1] Wesley called him 'that perfect disciple of his Lord'. He also became acquainted, probably in 1735, on the voyage to Georgia, with the Mexican hermit, Gregory Lopez (1542–96), who was a Spaniard born in Madrid. He went out to Mexico and from the age of twenty dedicated himself entirely to the pursuit of salvation. He lived as a recluse on a frugal diet, in a room which contained only a Bible, a globe and a pair of compasses. He managed, however, to master the works of St Teresa in twenty-four hours. His knowledge of the Bible became (not unnaturally) phenomenal, and although at first his private enterprise piety and his absence from mass made the hierarchy suspicious, he was renowned in his generation for supernatural wisdom and the pure love of God. Wesley was not blind to his limitations. He refers to him in his Journal as 'that good and wise, though much mistaken man'. But Wesley was haunted by the fact that Lopez's life became constant prayer, though this was to put the matter in its lowest terms. What Lopez experienced, as Wesley said in a letter, was 'an open intercourse' with God, 'a close, uninterrupted communion'.

Wesley transcribed the French Archbishop Fénelon's *Discourse on Simplicity* for a lady friend. Fénelon's teaching on Disinterested Love, that we should love God without seeking any reward, certainly not as a spiritual insurance policy, but for his own sake in response to his own love, entered into his awareness. So did the teaching of Madame Guyon, the French mystic, condemned by the Roman Church, who so influenced Fénelon, though Wesley would not accept her ignoring of the revelation of God in Christ,

nor her belief that union with God meant 'holy indifference' and the abolition of distinction between the soul and God. He would not go to her extremes in spite of the words of II Peter 1.4, that we should become 'partakers of the divine nature', on which he opened his Bible on 24 May 1738 and the many references in the hymns to our participation in the nature of God, 'lost in (his) immensity'.[2]

Influence of Thomas á Kempis

Ordination in 1725/6 was decisive in Wesley's life. He looked back on this period as the time when he gave himself totally to God. He was much affected by *The Imitation of Christ* of which he issued an edition 'compared with the original and corrected throughout' under the title *The Christian's Pattern: or A Treatise of the Imitation of Christ* in 1735, which was several times reprinted up to 1815.

Though it is most usually attributed to Thomas á Kempis (1380–1471), there are numerous contenders for its authorship. It is a highly derivative work which could have been written anywhere in Western Europe between the twelfth and fifteenth centuries. Dean Inge called it 'the ripe fruit of medieval theology as concentrated in the life of the cloister'. It had

---

2. I can't think that when God sent us into the world He had irreversibly decreed that we should be perpetually miserable in it ... What are become of all the innocent comforts and pleasures of life, if it is the intent of our Creator that we should never taste them? A fair patrimony indeed, which Adam has left his sons, if they are destined to be perpetually wretched!! ...

Another of his tenets, which is indeed a natural consequence of this is that all mirth is vain and useless if not sinful ... And he seems to carry the matter much too far on the other side afterwards, where he asserts that nothing is an affliction to a good man, and that he ought to thank God even for sending him misery.

Source: The Letters of the Rev John Wesley A M (8 vols) ed John Telford, Epworth Press 1931, Vol. I, pp. 15–16.

great influence on Ignatius Loyola, founder of the Jesuits, and on his *Spiritual Exercises*, but it was popular among Protestants as well as Catholics. Its tradition influenced Calvinist devotion and, as Helen White wrote, 'this thoroughly medieval work of mystical devotion serenely rode out all the storms of religious controversy of the three bitterest of modern Christian centuries'.[3]

It is divided into four parts – the Spiritual Life, the Inward Life, Internal Consolation and Holy Communion. The last two consist of a dialogue between Christ and a disciple. The *Imitation* does not follow the events of Christ's life and bid us imitate his actions, so much as seek the way of the Holy Cross and live the dying life of struggle and endurance with Christ and withdrawal into the inward, hidden life. Wesley said, 'I began to see that true religion was seated in the heart and that God's law extended to all our thoughts as well as our words and actions.' He felt, though, that á Kempis was too strict. On 28 May 1725, he wrote to his Mother on the subject[4] [2]. 'Holiness is happiness' was a favourite expression of the later Wesley. 'It is', says Martin Schmidt, 'rooted in a long English tradition'.[5] Wesley believes it even in these serious years. And á Kempis is very individualistic, contrary to Wesley's famous assertion that 'There is no holiness but social holiness.'

He may have been introduced to á Kempis by Sally Kirkham, one of the three daughters of the Rector of Stanton in the Cotswolds with whom he was in love and spent many happy hours and to whom his circle gave the name of Varanese. It was probably she who said that 'she would allow no one very young to read Dr Taylor of *Living and Dying*'. She added that he almost put her out of her senses when she was fifteen or sixteen years old, because 'he seemed to exclude all from being in a way of salvation who did not come up to his rules, some of which are altogether impracticable'.[6]

Yet, John Wesley could not avoid the severities of the gospel itself and he began to keep a rule based on Taylor [3].

3. 1 Begin and end every day with God and sleep not immoderately.
2 Be diligent in your calling.
3 Employ all spare hours in religion as able.
4 All holidays (holy days)
5 Avoid drunkards and busybodies.
6 Avoid curiosity and all useless employments and knowledge.
7 Examine yourself every night.
8 Never on any account pass any day without setting aside at least an hour for devotion.
9 Avoid all manner of passion.

Source: The Works of the Rev John Wesley AM ed T. Jackson (14 vols), Epworth Press 1829–31, Vol. VIII, p. 366.

Influence of William Law

Around 1729, Wesley read William Law's *Christian Perfection* and *A Serious Call to a Devout and Holy Life*. The latter had great influence on Dr Johnson, and, in the next century, John Keble. In some ways it foreshadowed the English novel with its character sketches. Law was a Non-Juror, one of those who separated from the Church of England because they could not accept William of Orange and the later Hanoverians since they had sworn allegiance to the Stuarts. John Wesley's mother, Susanna, was of this way of thinking as was the University of Oxford to which the Wesleys belonged. Law became influenced by Jacob Boehme or Behmen (1575–1624), a mystic whom Wesley condemned as totally obscure. Law was an enemy of formal religion. For him Christianity made inexorable demands. He taught Wesley to study the Bible and apply it to himself, to make it his 'frame of reference' for all the events, circumstances and decisions of his life.[7] He also accepted Law's belief that 'every man should consider himself a particular object of God's Providence; under the same care and protection of God as if the world had been made for him alone'.[8] And Wesley's famed teaching about 'the Catholic Spirit' is found in

William Law, that there is 'a communion of saints in the love of God and all goodness' which is not attained by orthodoxy in particular churches, but by a pure love of God, which creates a love of goodness and truth wherever it is found, even in faiths other than Christian. We must not 'work ourselves up into an abhorrence of a George Fox or Ignatius Loyola, but be equally glad of the light of the Gospel wherever it shines'.[9] After his evangelical conversion in 1738, Wesley wrote to Law with all a convert's arrogance and charged him with a Pharisaic doctrine of works and failure to understand that we are saved by God's initiative, not our own wearisome efforts. He rather repented of this later.

He became increasingly preoccupied with himself and his faults, idleness, by which he meant time spent in light reading rather than laziness, lying, boasting, greed of praise, heat in argument, detractions, that is running others down, intemperate sleep. Early rising became an obsession, over-indulgence in sleep a grave sin. This may have been due to sexual fantasies in dreams. Vivien Green has said that when he became a Fellow of Lincoln College, Oxford, in 1726, 'There was present a definite element of spiritual uncertainty, nor could he have stated what the future held in store.'[10] He was a conscientious don, better than many, but he probably became too concerned to convert his pupils to the ways of the Holy Club.

Early preaching and writing

On 1 January 1733, he preached a sermon before the University of Oxford which encapsulates the doctrine of his whole life. It was on 'The Circumcision of the Heart' (Rom. 2.29). Outward forms and observances are not the marks of the true followers of Christ, but rather 'a right state of soul', of mind and spirit, 'renewed after the true image of him that created it'. This is attained 'by humility, by faith in God, by joyful assurance, but also by a constant and continuing source of constant self-denial', and above all by love 'cutting off both the lust of the flesh, the lust of the eye and the pride of life', engaging the whole person in the ardent pursuit of God. 'Let your soul so be filled with so entire a love of him that you may love nothing but for his sake.' The teaching does not divide faith and works. The inspiration of both is God and the love of God.

In the same year Wesley published his first work *A Collection of Forms of Prayer for Every Day in the Week*. Originally for the Holy Club, and with prayers for the university prominent, it was regularly reissued with sometimes heavy revisions, throughout his life and beyond. It was included in the 1772 edition of his Works. It is mostly drawn from Non-Jurors, such as Nathaniel Spinckes, George Hickes and, it has been maintained, Robert Nelson, but they plagiarized from seventeenth-century authors, such as Lancelot Andrewes, William Laud and Thomas Ken. In his Preface Wesley says that the prayers are for those willing and able to spend half-an-hour twice a day for private devotion and who have 'a sincere reverence for, if not some acquaintance with, the ancient Christian Church'. The collectors had five aims [4], in the last one of which could be seen to be comprised the whole scheme of our Christian duty:

---

4. First, to have forms of prayer for every day of the week, each of which contained something of deprecation, petition, thanksgiving and intercession. Secondly, to have such forms for those days which the Christian Church has ever judged peculiarly proper for religious rejoicing as contained little of deprecation, but were explicit and large in acts of love and thanksgiving. Thirdly, to have such for those days which from the age of the apostles have been set apart for religious mourning as contained little of thanksgiving, but were full and express in acts of contrition and humiliation. Fourthly to have intercessions every day for all those whom our own Church directs us to remember in our prayers. And fifthly, to comprise in the course of petitions for the week, the whole scheme of our Christian duty.

Source: J. Wesley, Introduction to *Forms of Prayer* from a typescript of Frank Baker's in preparation for a forthcoming volume in the *Wesley Works* series (Nashville, Tennessee).

1. The renouncing of ourselves.
2. The devoting of ourselves to God whose we are.
3. Self-denial.
4. Mortification being crucified with Christ and dead to the world.
5. 'Christ liveth in me, being alive to God'.

The sequel is well known. After his father's death, John Wesley and his younger brother, Charles, went out to Georgia to minister to the colonists and hopefully to convert the Indians. In both their cases this was something of a disaster, though John did some good.

The Wesleys in Georgia

In Georgia John Wesley turned to the mystics, though he did not know the great Carmelites of the sixteenth century, St Teresa and St John of the Cross. But the mediaeval Tauler and the French Antoinette Bourignon and Molinos's *Spiritual Guide* (1675) did not appeal to him. They verged on heresy, were in danger of dispensing with the incarnation, and offered the immediacy of communion with God, which he was seeking, at the price of a solitary, introspective religion which was dangerous for his sociable nature and possibly derogated the second commandment, love of neighbour. His language was vehement at this period: 'All the other enemies of Christ are triflers – the mystics are the most dangerous of its enemies.'

He countered the mystics by further study of the fathers. One of these was known as 'Macarius the Egyptian'. Wesley was to include extracts from his homilies in the first volume of *The Christian Library*. During a stormy voyage in Georgia, he wrote, 'I read Macarius and sang.' Scholarship has now made it likely that this 'Macarius' was no Egyptian 'desert father' but a fifth-century Syrian monk, whose conception of Christian spirituality was derived from Gregory of Nyssa, 'the greatest of all the Eastern teachers of the quest for perfection'.[11] Outler argues

that this means that the young Wesley was influenced by Orthodox monasticism and that his teaching about perfection was thereby saved from certain Roman and sectarian faux-pas. Perfection for him was never a moral state which could not be improved, it was a life of constant growth in disciplined love to God and man. Through his reading of Macarius, Wesley absorbed the writings of Gregory [5]. To quote Macarius: 'It is only gradually that a man grows and comes to a perfect man, to the measure of the stature, not, as some would say "Off with one coat and on with another."'[12] Wesley did not always give the impression of such wisdom.

---

5. This truly is the vision of God: never to be satisfied in the desire to see him. But one must always, by looking at what he can see, rekindle his desire to see more. Thus, no limit would interrupt growth in the ascent to God, since no limit to the Good can be found nor is the increasing of desire for the Good brought to an end because it is satisfied.

Source: Malherbe and Ferguson (eds), *Gregory of Nyssa*, SPCK 1978, p. 116.

Wesley also admired the later fathers of both East and West, Chrysostom, Basil, Jerome, Augustine, 'and above all that man of a broken heart, Ephraem Syrus (306–373)',[13] who had a legendary reputation in the Middle East and Edessa. He was an outstandingly original religious poet. He has been called, by the Roman Catholic scholar, A. G. Mortimort, 'the real father of Christian hymnography'. His poems, Nicene orthodoxy in metre, allowed congregations to participate by singing the refrains of the stanzas into which the poems could be divided.[14] Though the form of his spirituality was entirely Syrian and therefore more semitic than Greek, he belongs to the Eastern school of perfectionism like 'Macarius'. His theological insights are similar to those of the so-called Cappadocian fathers, Basil of Caesaria, and the two Gregorys, Nyssa and Nazianzus, who were his contemporaries. His poetry abounds with clothing imagery. 'At the Fall, Adam and Eve lost the "robe of glory" with which they had originally been clothed; to remedy this situation God the Word "put on the body of Adam/humanity" at his baptism, depositing in Jordan the "robe of glory" for humanity to put on again, in Christian baptism.' Baptism is the 'potential re-entry' into paradise, but a paradise far more glorious than Eden, 'since Adam/humanity will there attain to divinity'. This is the work of the Divine love; and God has revealed himself not only in the Incarnation, that focal point of time, but in scripture and nature too. The Christian life transfigures the material world. 'The model of the relationship between creation and Creator is continuously present in the eucharist.'[15] Notice that the baptism rather than the birth or conception of Jesus is the event by which the Son of God took our nature upon him.

Wesley had encountered Moravian refugees on the voyage to Georgia. The Moravians are spiritual descendants of the smothered sects who opposed Rome in the Middle Ages, of the Bohemian Brethren and John Hus, but they owed their eighteenth-century importance to the leadership of their benefactor, Count Zinzendorf, who received them as immigrants on one of his estates in Saxony, Herrnhut. From here they established themselves both in America and England. Liturgy was central to their church life, the expression of their creed, but they had, imparted by Zinzendorf, a strongly evangelical tenderness, not unlike Catholic devotion, to the wounds and sacred heart of Jesus. They were disciples, direct or indirect, of Molinos, and there was peace and quiet in their devotion and activity. Wesley was impressed by their calm during an Atlantic storm on the way to Georgia. They sang hymns while he and most others cowered in fear.

They had strong affinities with the Lutherans, with whom they had sought, unsuccessfully, to make common cause and they brought this dimension into Wesley's spirituality. The day after he landed in America, Wesley met their Bishop Spangenberg, who asked him directly if he had the 'witness of the Spirit' described in Romans 8.16f., and also 'Do you know Jesus Christ?' Wesley replied, 'I know that he is the Saviour of the world', but Spangenberg pressed him. 'True, but do you know that he has saved you?' Wesley could merely say, 'I hope he has died to save me.'

Return to London

He returned to London at the end of 1737 in a state of despair after his bungled love affair with Sophy Hopkey, his refusal to give her and the man she had married holy communion, and general unpopularity because of his high churchmanship. He met a Moravian, Peter Böhler, who made him feel that he was still unconverted and ignorant of the Saviour. What is remarkable is that in spite of his uncertainties, he was preaching with renewed power and already giving offence to staid, formal church people. Some London pulpits became closed to him. He himself wondered whether he should continue through lack of faith. But Böhler countered him wisely in words which have become famous: 'Preach faith *till* you have it; and then *because* you have it you *will* preach faith.'

He was also going regularly to Evensong at St Paul's Cathedral. The influence of the Book of Common Prayer and the Church of England Homilies must not be underestimated, suffused as they are with the Protestant conviction that we are saved by faith in the once-for-all sacrifice of Christ and, in spite of our manifold sins, freely forgiven. The Prayer Book is charged today with being over-weighted with penitence. Such critics have never read the penitentials of Celtic Christianity, which is held up as an ascetic system with much to teach us. It is easy to ignore the lives which people of the sixteenth century – and since – lived in the world, though when, decades later, Wesley abridged its communion rite for his Sunday Service for America, he did remove from the confession of our sins the words 'the burden of them is intolerable'.

The 'second journey'

It was a few months after his return from Georgia that, on 24 May 1738, he went in the evening 'very unwillingly' to the meeting of a religious society in Aldersgate Street and as someone was reading from Luther's Preface to the Epistle to the Romans, he felt his heart 'strangely warmed' and received something of the assurance for which he had been seeking.

This was the start of his 'second journey'. Father Gerald O'Collins has traced this phenomenon in many lives, Paul, Augustine, Ignatius Loyola, John Henry Newman, as well as John Wesley, the most famous. Through some outward circumstance, disturbance of a settled life, sickness, or second conversion, the whole of life is changed. It is lived in a different milieu, with different activities and relationships. Old associations and friendships are discontinued, the lifestyle is altered. So it was with Wesley after 1738.[16] He may sometimes in occasional bouts of despair have wished for Oxford again, but the academic life was abandoned, the pleasurable social relationships faded away. His associations were often from the pits, if not the gutter, rather than the senior common room and the parlour. His time was spent with his evangelical converts whom he sought to lead to Christlikeness, to perfect love. He attempted this by uniting the spirituality of his past reading and rule of life to the experience of men and women out of the common way. This led to some excesses and dangers, but at its best it created a spirituality which we may claim as ecumenical. The evidence for this is *The Christian Library* in fifty volumes. This contains abridgments of the Apostolic Fathers, English Puritans (in large measure), High Churchmen, Cambridge Platonists, Scots such as Scougal, Leighton and Rutherford, Pascal, Fénelon, Molinos, and the aforementioned Mexican hermit, Gregory Lopez.

For discussion

1. 'Holiness is happiness': is this compatible with the command to take up the Cross, or with acts of 'religious mourning' prescribed in *Forms of Prayer*?

2. Read *Hymns and Psalms*, No. 282. Does it have any meaning for you?

3. Do you accept what William Law says about being a particular object of God's Providence?

4. Have you had experience of the 'second journey'?

5. List the influences which have formed your spirituality. Have people of the present or the past been most influential, books, sermons or personal encounters?

2

Rapture and Order : 'Our Hymns' and 'Our Discipline'

Methodist spirituality as it developed in Wesley's lifetime was 'a psalm of praise' for God's free grace, proclaimed in the hymn of that title [6], consequent on the Wesleys' experience of 1738 being imparted to thousands of men and women. It united Oxford dons and the worst criminals. It abolished any distinctions of human virtue, or rank. 'All have sinned and come short of the glory of God.' But there is mercy for all. 'The vilest offender may turn and find grace.' Condemned criminals in Newgate have a hope of salvation greater than the human pardon they have been denied. Thus the poor man condemned of robbing his master could discover that none other than the Son of God had borne terrible sufferings and died for him.

---

6.   And can it be that I should gain
     An interest in the Saviour's blood?
     Died he for me who caused his pain?
     For me who him to death pursued?
     Amazing love! how can it be
     That thou my God shouldst die for me!

Source: *A Collection of Hymns for the Use of The People called Methodists*, 1780, No. 193.

'Sing faith till you have it'

The rapture was both expressed and contained by being sung in hymns. These are inseparable from Methodist devotion. The 1780 Collection encapsulates Methodist spirituality. The contents of that hymnbook describe the journey of the soul. After 'exhorting and beseeching to return to God' there is a description of the pleasantness of religion, the goodness of God, death, judgment, heaven, hell. Formal and inward religion are then described, followed by prayers for repentance. There are hymns for mourners convinced of sin and brought to the birth, for those convinced of backsliding – a recurrent danger – and their recovery, and then for believers, rejoicing, fighting, praying, watching, working, suffering, groaning for full redemption brought to birth, saved and interceding for the world. The fifth part is for the Society, meeting, giving thanks, praying, parting.[1]

There is a contrast with the contents of Newton and Cowper's *Olney Hymns*, published in the previous year, which was intended to have seven sections [7], but to which was added at the last moment an eighth section of short hymns suitable for the liturgy.

---

7. Newton's arrangement is less elaborate and follows the basic pattern of his letters on growth in grace. The sinner is first awakened to contrition and spiritual desire (1: Solemn Addresses to Sinners; 2: Seeking, Pleading, Hoping) before experiencing testing (3: Conflict) which, intermingled with divine assistance (4: Comfort) leads to a more perfect obedience and resignation to God (5: Dedication and Surrender; 6: Cautions), leading in time to a more contemplative frame of mind focussed on Christ (7: Praise).

Source: Bruce Hindmarsh: *John Newton and English Evangelical Religion*, Clarendon Press 1996, p. 271, summarizing contents of *Olney Hymns* Book 3, 1779.

The Wesleys, of course, had hymns, not included in the Collection, on the great doctrines of faith, what J. E. Rattenbury characterized as 'Hymns of the Hinterland' complementing the 'Hymns of the Pilgrim Way'.[2] There were also the *Hymns on the Lord's Supper*, of which more later.

The influence of hymns on Methodism cannot be exaggerated. They gave its devotion a lyrical quality. The best may be considered true poetry.[3] They belong to a dimension beyond the simply rational and fixed in their singers' minds concepts of faith, doctrine and experience unattained by prosaic ratiocination. Newman said in the next century, 'Poetry does not address the reason, but the imagination and affections.' Later, the Irish poet W. B. Yeats said that poetry is not a criticism of life 'but a revelation of a hidden life'. It has 'ability to initiate the chosen in the great secret which is all embracing, is mysterious and only to be understood by the few', though the Wesleys were concerned with the many and loved the multitude praising God. Not all would attain the heights and depths and the intimate knowledge the hymns made possible, but the revelation was open to all. The hymns made Christian theology available to those far from the schools. It became part of their persona. And the hymns were used in private devotion as well as congregational worship. This was probably true of all the hymns of the eighteenth century, Watts and Doddridge as well as Olney, where they were sung and expounded in prayer meetings. Some Wesley hymns are almost too personal, too intimate for a mixed congregation, though the Wesleys' attitude may have been 'Sing faith till you have it', while the singing of the hymns made the spirituality the Methodists' own, engraved the sentiments on their hearts, as prose without music would not have done. It is true, though, that beauty is shy, poetry is like a vest of modesty, which may seem in contrast with raucous Methodism and even Charles Wesley, who in Gordon Rupp's words sang his hymns with such 'roaring confidence' that brought 'on one occasion at least a protest from local inhabitants in a world before the noise pollution of jet aircraft and transistor radio'. The fathers of the Oxford

Movement next century, unlike their Anglo-Catholic successors, would fear that hymn-singing and much evangelical practice cheapened the divine mysteries. It rather brought them into the lives of the common people, without tearing away the veil completely, though perhaps wonder rather than awe was the Methodist response. Not all Methodist hymns were noisy and intended to drown the cries of riotous opponents. One of the hymns about the Great Feast has as the climax of gospel benefits

> The speechless awe that dares not move
> And all the silent heaven of love.[4]

John Wesley found it necessary to give *Directions for Singing* in 1761. The tunes he prescribed must be learned first and all the hymn must be sung. Methodists must sing lustily, modestly ('Do not bawl'), sing in time, above all sing spiritually. 'Have an eye to God in everything that you sing ... see that your heart is not carried away with the sound, but offered to God continually.'[5]

This is very much of the spirit of the Lutheran martyr of 1945, Dietrich Bonhoeffer, who wrote in *Life Together*, a book for his illicit Seminary under the Nazis, some paragraphs on 'Singing the new song' [8]. There was also discipline. Ronald Knox

---

8. The heart sings because it is overflowing with Christ (very Wesleyan). That is why all singing in Church is a spiritual performance ... There is no place in the service of worship where vanity and bad taste can intrude as in the singing. There is the solo voice that goes swaggering, swelling, blaring and tremulant from a full chest and drowns out everything else to the glory of its own fine organ ... there are often those who because of some mood will not join in the singing and thus disturb the fellowship. The more we sing, the more joy we will derive from it, but, above all, the more devotion and discipline and joy we put into our singing the richer will be the blessing that will come to the whole life of the fellowship from singing together.

Source: Dietrich Bonhoeffer, *Life Together*, SCM Press 1954, pp. 48ff.

wrote that Wesley's 'ideal did not fall short of persuading 70,000 people to adopt, for all practical purposes, the rules of the Holy Club'.[6]

Societies, bands and classes

Wesley organized his converts into Societies, on the model of the Religious Societies of the time and these he divided into 'bands' and, later, 'classes'. As early as Christmas Day 1739, he drew up rules for the former.

They are based on the injunction of the letter of James, 'Confess your faults one to another and pray for one another that ye may be healed.' The meetings are to be at least weekly, punctuality is mandatory, and there is to be total frankness in the confession of faults and the mutual telling of them 'plain and home'. Cases of conscience are to be brought and resolved. The method is close questioning, as was that of all the meetings Wesley instituted. Five years later, on Christmas Day 1744, Wesley listed 'Directions to the Band Societies'. These are first to abstinence from evil; no trade on the sabbath, no spirituous liquors except medicinally, no pawning of goods, 'no, not to save a life', no mention of faults behind a person's back, no needless ornaments, or self-indulgence, such as tobacco, or snuff. Secondly, they are to good works: almsgiving, frugality, diligence, loving reproval of evil; and thirdly, fidelity to all the ordinances of God; weekly church attendance and communion, presence at five o'clock preaching every morning, daily prayer and scripture and Friday fasts.

The classes, considered a distinctive feature of Methodism and still to some extent in being, came into existence more by improvisation. A financial levy on members of Society was necessary and a member in Bristol thought that this was best collected by a weekly meeting. Wesley agreed and saw the spiritual possibilities. The discipline of the class meeting was less rigid than that of the bands but it was none the less strict and obligatory. The purpose is well summed up in a hymn by Charles Wesley, the first verse from the Prayer Book version of Psalm 139.23f. [9].

Detractors thought that the class meetings were closet confessionals, or covens of Jesuits, or even, in early years, undercover Jacobites. The Roman Catholic Bishop Challoner appreciated these aspersions even less than the Methodists and damned Methodist preachers as ministers of Satan, false prophets, and wolves in sheep's clothing.[7]

The Societies were not left in isolation in the places in which they were formed. They became linked together in Circuits ministered to by travelling preachers who were not supposed to remain for more than a short time – a year or even in early days, a quarter. Wesley thought that they would have 'preached their congregations asleep' by then. The Circuits became a nation-wide 'Connexion' under a Conference of the travelling preachers, whose authority, with Wesley in the chair, was supreme.

This system had considerable effects on spirituality. Circuits enabled mutual help among the Societies and a sharing of resources. The itinerant ministry

---

9.   Try us, O God, and search the ground
      Of every sinful heart.
      What e'er of sin in us is found,
      O bid it all depart.

      When to the right or left we stray,
      Leave us not comfortless!
      But guide our feet into the way
      Of everlasting peace.

      Help us to help each other, Lord,
      Each other's cross to bear
      Let each his friendly aid afford,
      And feel his brother's care.

      Help us to build each other up,
      Our little stock improve;
      increase our faith, confirm our hope,
      And perfect us in love.

Source: 1780 Collection, No. 489.

made possible a variety of gifts, so that the members were not subject for years on end to one preaching and pastoral style. There was, most important, the fact that the itinerant came from outside the local Society, represented the Connexion and would in time make the local bodies part of a world church, their gaze lifted above the parochial. There was also a central authority, which some have compared to the Vatican, legislating for the whole Connexion. Wesley thought of Methodists as an order within the Church of England, though this was not practicable amid Anglican hostility and the lack of loyalty among many of Wesley's converts to the English Church. In the 1740s, Wesley contemplated a distinctive dress for his members and they were to eschew adornments. The sexes were segregated. There was to be no self-indulgence in singing lush tunes, for instance, and the nub of Methodist spirituality, 'the glory of Methodism', was the preaching at five o'clock in the morning. Yet this went with a certain theological and doctrinal tolerance. Various 'opinions' could be held and granted a basic adherence to the historic creeds and the truths of scripture, there could be differences about church order, and indeed those matters on which Milton's fallen angels had disputed, 'free will, fixed fate, foreknowledge absolute', though this was less allowable in the light of the most bitter disputes with the Calvinists in the 1770s. Nor would Wesley allow Anglican Methodists to go to Dissenters' meetings. But his slogan was, 'Though we cannot think alike, may we not love alike?' The Order for the pursuit of holiness could be transdenominational, provided no disciplines were breached.

For discussion

1. Do the contents of the 1780 *Collection* describe your spiritual pilgrimage ?

2. Do you and your congregation enjoy 'lush tunes' and is there spiritual danger in this? Are some tunes unChristian; if so why?

3. Does an emphasis on singing hymns exclude those who, like C. S. Lewis, cannot stand them, or the tone deaf, or the young today whose idea of music is different and who do not find inspiration in community singing as much as in groups or individual performances?

4. Most Christian women today wear jewellery, earrings for instance, and make-up and dress fashionably. John Wesley and William Law might not approve. Are they justified, are there real dangers, or does attractive dress 'adorn the Gospel'?

5. Are there spiritual dangers in Wesley's directions for the band and class meetings?

3

The Means of Grace :
Meditation and Mysticism

Wesley carefully enumerates the 'means of grace' by which holiness is to be attained. They are divided into the 'instituted 'and the 'prudential'. The former include

1. Prayer: private, family, public.
2. Searching the scriptures, by reading, meditating and hearing.

For meditation he went to Puritan models. In an alternative version of his advice to helpers, he wrote: 'Meditating: At set times? How? By Bishop Hall's or Mr Baxter's rule? How long?'[1]

Joseph Hall

Joseph Hall (1574–1656) was a Bishop of Exeter and Norwich who advocated moderation between Calvinists and Arminians, favoured the Puritans but was imprisoned for defending the Church of England against a hostile Parliament in 1640. He published *The Arte of Meditation* in 1606. He describes meditation as 'the ladder of heaven ... and the best improvement of Christianity' and draws on monastic, patristic, mediaeval and fifteenth and sixteenth-century continental and Catholic sources. He is undoubtedly influenced by Ignatius Loyola's *Spiritual Exercises* although he has more sympathy with Augustine's emphasis on the priority of God's grace than spiritual techniques. Meditation does cross the boundaries between Catholic and Protestant.[2]

Hall defines meditation as 'The bending of the mind upon some spiritual object, through divers forms of discourse, until our thoughts come to an issue.' It is concerned with knowledge, but, above all, with affection, which latter is what Hall wants to see kindled in his own time.

Meditation begins in the understanding and should end in the affection. He describes how one should choose a subject, organize and classify it. He has a meditation on death. A modern version might look something like this:

We think of death as the end of life, a terrible finality, the bourne from which no traveller returns, and yet it may be release, freedom from the limitations of mortality, the burdens of this life. It is in some sense necessary in our human life, to growth. The adult cannot exist unless the child dies. And if we are fully to enter into God's kingdom it can only be through death. And death may be the supreme act of love. We can show the greatest love for our friends and indeed our enemies by dying for them. This does not necessarily mean martyrdom or deliberate laying down of our lives. The very fact of our mortal passage makes room for future generations and should be thought of as a means of loving them and giving them their opportunities in this world, above all their opportunity to know God.

Having thus sought to understand death, in so far as that is possible, we might think of examples of the way people have died, particularly Christians from the martyrs on. We then should think of Christ's victory over death and the hope beyond the grave and the quality of the life we have in him. We do not deserve it, but it is offered through his free grace We may die and rise with him. Baptism is the promise of this. But have we improved, renewed it? Or do we live as though Christ had never died and risen again?[3]

This exercise of the affections Hall compares to tasting what we have seen (Ps. 34.8), but we see by the understanding before we taste, by the affections. It will, however, bring us to penitence as well as praise.

Hall thought that meditation should be solitary. Its subject should be, as a rule, a great Christian doctrine, or some aspect of the life of Christ or, as we have tried to show, some decisive, fateful human experience.[4]

Richard Baxter

Richard Baxter (1615-91) was the greatest of the Puritans, an outstanding pastor, who sought for the reconciliation of all Christians. *The Saint's Everlasting Rest,* which Wesley reissued, is possibly the greatest of all treatises on Meditation.[5] It gives a lengthy account of set or solemn meditation. This begins with Consideration or Cogitation, active spiritual reasoning. The matter on which this must work is produced by the memory (doubtless aided by a notebook!) which furnishes suitable scriptural passages and promises, articles of the creed, or extracts from spiritual writings. These should be stored over the years. The rational judgment then examines the promise contained in the passage chosen. This will often result in questioning and argument – doubt has its place in meditation – in order to bring conviction of the truth of scripture or tradition, but the mind's assent to this must be turned into positive and personal assurance that the general promise of God is all related to my everlasting joy.

Next, the affections must be kindled in love, desire, hope, courage and joy – all to be inflamed by consideration of the chosen passage. And so we pass to a further stage, soliloquy, 'which is nothing but a

pleading the case with our own souls', 'a preaching to one's self'. This is likely to lead to reproof and penitence and prayer, speaking sometimes to oneself and sometimes to God. The Psalms are patterns of soliloquy. Prayer, 'which is a weightier duty than most are aware of', is the climax of meditation.

This careful and solemn exercise will obviously lead sometimes to an 'ecstatic pause' as we glimpse something of the glories of the kingdom of God. But special insights and graces apart, it will help us towards that goal which Charles Wesley desired:

> O that my every breath were praise
> O that my heart were filled with God![6]

It may at times end in aridity and heaviness; of this Wesley was not perhaps sufficiently aware. John Haime, a soldier at the battle of Dettingen in 1743, under fire for several hours, found his heart 'filled with love, joy and peace more than tongue could express'. He testified to others having seen more of the glory of God when grievously wounded in battle that at any time in their lives. But after three years of conscious communion with God, he passed through a period of despair which lasted for twenty. Wesley was puzzled by this as a Catholic would not have been.[7]

False or true mysticism?

We have mentioned his opposition to mysticism[8] increased by the 'stillness' which caused his separation from the Moravians in the early 1740s. They believed that one should avoid the means of grace until sanctified. Wesley's own approach to building up the soul [10] was different from that of Bishop Hall, who leant towards solitary meditation. But Ronald Knox cherished the belief that 'there was in Wesley something of the mystic; that his bent, if Providence had not seen fit to order his career otherwise, was towards a solitary, a contemplative life.[9] Knox does not give sufficient weight to that Journal entry en route for Georgia in which Wesley says that

10. The Mystics' manner of building up souls is quite opposite to that prescribed by Christ. They advise 'To the desert! to the desert! and God will build you up', whereas according to the Judgement of our Lord and the writings of the Apostles, it is only when we are knit together that we have nourishment from him. The religion these authors would edify us in is a solitary religion. Directly opposite to this is the Gospel of Christ . . . Solitary religion is not found there . . . The Gospel of Christ knows of no religion but social. There is no holiness but social holiness.

Source: George Osborn (ed), *Poetical Works of John and Charles Wesley*, London 1868–72, Introduction to Vol. I.

for years he had thought he needed solitude in order to be a Christian. Now he has solitude enough, but is not therefore a better Christian. There was a tension between the mystic way and what at this time was his Moravian friends' insistence on evangelical conversion. Wesley was led to the latter. It is ironic that the Moravians who had pointed him to justification by faith alone, and thereby to the English Reformers and away from William Law with his leanings towards Jacob Boehme, should prove to be the most dangerously mystical of all. They provoked him in 1743 to his most intemperate language against the mystic writers 'whom I declare in my cool judgment and in the presence of the Most High God, I believe to be the one great anti-Christ'. He never took kindly to some of the mystical hymns of his brother Charles and omitted 'Thou shepherd of Israel and mine' from the 1780 *Collection*. His sermon on 'The Wilderness State' seems in part to be an attack on the mystics' doctrine of the dark night of the soul, hence his puzzlement over John Haime. But there is a mystical element in his spirituality. We have noted above his reading in such as Madame Guyon, an extract from whose life he issued in 1776, and Molinos and William Law, and that he was willing for his preachers to read them too. He taught Methodists to sing his translations of Paul Gerhardt and Tersteegen and Antoinete Bourignon. He tempered some of his earlier criticisms, and from 1765 deleted the sentence

about anti-Christ from all editions of his Journal. There are signs that the influence of John Fletcher helped him to evaluate the mystics more justly. In Letter V to Richard Hill in the fourth of his *Checks to Antinomianism*, Fletcher distinguishes between false mysticism and the true mysticism of scripture, which furthers 'the deep mysteries of inward religion', and hopes that in future Mr Wesley will do the same.[10]

There can be no doubt that Charles Wesley's mysticism could be dangerous. In the 1740 original version of the hymn on Hebrews 4.9, 'Lord I believe a rest remains', the last lines are these:

> Let all I am in thee be lost
> Let all I am be God.

And there are other lines:

> Make my soul thy pure abode
> Fill with all the deity,
> Swallowed up and lost in God.

This may be an instance in Methodism of the Eastern Orthodox doctrine of deification, but whereas the Orthodox are careful to distinguish between the essence and the energies of God and maintain that Christians may attain to the latter, his goodness and active love rather than his inmost being, Charles Wesley prays 'Fill with all the deity'.

Other hymns are safer. Newton Flew, who with Rattenbury and others regarded 'Thou shepherd of Israel and mine' from Song of Songs 1.7. as 'one of the unapproachable lyrics of devotion', has shown how its mysticism is compatible with the New Testament in that it does not open the door to a confusion between the creature and the Creator, that it is saved from mere individualism and does not contemplate any rest or bliss which cannot be shared, and that the centre and object of its devotion is Christ crucified.[11]

Henry Bett, who sought to rescue John Wesley from the charge that he regarded mysticism as simply folly and that for him religion was devoid of mystery, cites his regard for Antoinette de Bourignon and Madame Guyon, and his brother's hymn 'Come, Holy Ghost, all-quickening fire'[11].

---

11. Eager for thee I ask and pant,
    So strong the principle divine,
Carries me out with sweet constraint
    Till all my hallowed soul is thine;
Plunged in the Godhead's deepest sea
    And lost in thine immensity.

Source: 1780 *Collection*, No. 363.

Charles Wesley borrowed from William Law and Jacob Boehme the notion that the regenerate soul is a 'transcript of the Trinity'. The new birth means that all three persons are born in the heart to restore the Divine image of the humanity of God's creation.[12]

For discussion

1. Do you find meditation essential to your prayer? How do you go about it? Do you take a passage of scripture and make a three-point sermon to yourself out of it?

2. Is it possible to make a meditation which leads you to God out of something other than scripture – a reading from elsewhere, an incident, an observation, even an advertisement?

3. Is there a danger of meditation becoming too cerebral, too much 'mental prayer'? Does it become wearisome and arid, so that we need simply to rest in the Lord by contemplation for relief? Or does it naturally lead to contemplation being 'lost in wonder, love and praise?' Or do you begin with contemplation, music, poetry, the sounds of nature, and rest in the realities you know?

4. Have you had an experience which you would describe as 'mystical', a sense of the presence of God, or Christ, and of union with him?

4

The Means of Grace: The Lord's Supper

To return to the instituted means of grace. The third is the Lord's Supper, which must be received at every opportunity. For the Wesleys the injunction of Christ was supreme: 'Do this in remembrance of me.'

> If Jesus bids me lick the dust
> I bow to his command.

'Is not the eating of that bread, and the drinking of that cup, the outward visible means whereby God conveys into our souls all the spiritual grace, that righteousness, and peace, and joy in the Holy Ghost, which were purchased by the body of Christ once broken and the blood of Christ once shed for us?'[1]

The Methodist revival was something of a sacramental revival in that the Wesleys presided over crowded communion services, unknown in the church at that time, and wished for more frequent communion than was customary when perhaps three or four times a year was the norm. They seem to have believed that daily communion was the early church custom. John Wesley once received the sacrament on each of the twelve days of Christmas. The last of the *Hymns on the Lord's Supper* prays 'restore the daily Sacrifice' and implies that this will herald the coming of the kingdom.

John Wesley thought of the Lord's Supper as a 'converting' as well as a 'confirming' ordinance. The disciples were not converted when they first received it in the Upper Room and many who came to the Table could receive a deeper experience of grace and make a more absolute commitment than before. The Supper was 'the choicest instrument of grace' [12].

---

12. The Prayer, the Fast, the Word conveys,
    When mixed with Faith, thy Life to me,
    In all the Channels of thy Grace
    I still have fellowship with thee.
    But chiefly here my soul is fed
    With Fullness of Immortal Bread.

Source : Hymns on the Lord's Supper, No. 54.

Hymns on the Lord's Supper

The *Hymns on the Lord's Supper* (1745), the best-seller of all Wesleys' collections, were intended to be sung during the lengthy distribution of the elements at those thronged services. They are largely a paraphrase of *The Christian Sacrament and Sacrifice* (1672) of Daniel Brevint (1616–95), an extract from which prefaces them. There are as well unhappy bowdlerizations of George Herbert's 'The Invitation' and 'The Banquet', and, more important, several echoes of the fourth-century *Apostolic Constitutions* (e.g. No. 16), a church order which, in the eighteenth-century, some believed to date from the apostles.

Brevint was a Jersey man and an exile in France during the Commonwealth, where he chose Anglicanism as an alternative both to Rome and French Protestantism. He was already a French Reformed Pastor, with a degree incorporated at Oxford after some dispute. He received Anglican orders in Paris, and became chaplain to the wife and daughter of the great French Marshall Turenne. He first wrote *The Christian Sacrament and Sacrifice* for them in French. Charles II met him in Paris, and on his return to England at the Restoration he was given the living of Brancepeth in Durham and became a Prebendary. He was made Dean of Lincoln in 1681. It will be noted that the Wesleys were Lincolnshire men.

A thorough analysis of these hymns would be an imbalance, but we may note certain characteristics which, in spite of some of the blood-soaked language with which a modern congregation would not feel happy, make the hymns of ecumenical significance in our time, in writings such as those of C. H. Dodd, or Dom Odo Casel (d.1947). The sacrament takes us back to calvary, or brings it into the present, so that we are there.

> Crucified before our eyes
> Where we our maker see.[2]
>
> Now let (Faith) pass the years between.
> And view thee bleeding on the tree
> My God who dies for me, for me.[3]

It is the Lord's death we show forth and Calvary which is the locus of our devotion, whereas many today think of remembrance as including the resurrection and the eucharist as a meal with the risen Christ. But the eighteenth century, as is evidenced by Watts' communion hymn, 'When I survey the wondrous Cross', was firmly in the Western mediaeval and Prayer Book tradition, and that of Paul, you 'proclaim the Lord's death until he comes'. This is pivotal to faith. It is perennial. God is always as Christ on Calvary. 'Thou stand'st the ever-slaughtered Lamb'.[4] Calvary is cause for rejoicing as well as mourning.

There is great emphasis on sacrifice. The sacrifice of Christ is once-for-all and can never be repeated, but by remembering it, we are proclaiming it and thus re-presenting it.

It is important to note, however, that the hymn of which this verse [13] forms a part has never been included in the section on the sacraments of any Methodist hymnbook since 1745, including 1983. In

---

13. With solemn Faith we offer up,
    And spread before thy glorious Eyes
    that only Ground of all our Hope,
    that precious, bleeding Sacrifice,
    Which brings thy Grace on Sinners down,
    And perfects all our Souls in One.

Source: *Hymns on the Lord's Supper*, No. 125.

---

the 1780 *Collection*, it is in the section, 'For Believers brought to Birth'.

Brevint says 'too many Christians live as if under the Gospel there were no sacrifice but that of Christ on the Cross'. Wesley insists that the whole church is a sacrifice offered with Christ [14]. 'Christ and his Church are one' (See *Hymns on the Lord's Supper*, No. 129). There is also individual consecration, as in a hymn to the Trinity [15], which may have influenced Frances Ridley Havergal's more widely-sung hymn from the next century, 'Take my life and let it be'.

---

14. Would the Saviour of Mankind
    Without his people die?
    No to Him we all are join'd
    As more than Standers by.
    Freely as the Victim came
    To the Altar of His Cross,
    We attend the Slaughter'd Lamb
    And suffer for His Cause.

Source: *Hymns on the Lord's Supper*, No. 131.

---

15. Take my Soul and Body's Powers,
    Take my Mem'ry, Mind and Will,
    All my Goods, and all my Hours,
    All I know and all I feel,
        All I think and speak and do;
    Take my heart, but make it new.

Source: *Hymns on the Lord's Supper*, No. 158.

The sacrament is a pledge of heaven [16]. Wesley more than Brevint uses the word 'taste' to describe it. This, says Geoffrey Wainwright, is much rarer in eucharistic liturgies and theologies than one might have expected, but its value as an expression for the relation between the 'already' and the 'not yet' is undeniable.[5]

---

16.   He gives our souls a taste
        Heaven into our hearts He pours.

Source: Hymns on the Lord's Supper, No. 103.

Charles Wesley does use the metaphor of taste elsewhere. In the section 'For Believers Rejoicing' in the 1780 *Collection* there is a hymn (No. 197) first published in 1749 in 'Hymns and Sacred Poems', which exults in the possession of Christ and dances to the sound of Jesus' name:

Yet onward I haste, to the heavenly feast;
That, that is the fullness, but this is the taste.

There is no mention of the Lord's Supper, any more than in the Conversion hymn where forgiveness is called 'this antepast of heaven' (1780 *Collection*, No. 29) But, clearly, the metaphor is particularly appropriate to the eating and drinking of communion [17]. The Saviour himself has *tasted* death (*Hymns on the Lord's Supper*, No. 100), eaten the bread of affliction and drunk the cup of God's wrath. He has thereby departed from our sight into heaven, but has left behind his sacramental pledge, to which we will hold on until his return in the clouds. This will be our welcome home, received into the arms of the Friend of sinners, who, when he knew he was going to die and was offering himself totally to God, pledged himself to his disciples in the supper. And this we shall ever recall in heaven.

The metaphor of the pledge recurs in the hymns as does the translation of the Greek *arrabon*, earnest, though Brevint points out that an earnest is part of a promised payment which will be received in full later, whereas a pledge is not needed once it is fulfilled. So the graces God bestows in his sacraments are an earnest of what will remain and be completed in the happiness of heaven, while 'the Sacraments themselves shall be taken back and shall no more appear in heaven than the cloudy pillar in Canaan'.

The supper fulfils the prayer of John 17 that Christ's disciples may be perfected in One, which is the life of heaven. It unites the church on earth and in heaven (*Hymns on the Lord's Supper*, No. 96) It enables us to behold the dazzling company, 'saints and angels joined in one' which stand before God's throne (*Hymns on the Lord's Supper*, No. 105). The saints begin the Gloria and the morning stars reply in an antiphon of praise. The angels pay homage, at first prostrate in silence, but then they join the hymn in a mighty shout of praise.

---

17.   How glorious is the life above,
        Which in this ordinance we taste
            What fulness of celestial love
        The joy which shall forever last!

Source: Hymns on the Lord's Supper, No. 101.

The sacrament is the place of meeting with the departed. No psychic sessions or medium's contact are needed. Hymn 106 is a paraphrase of Revelation 7.13–17, 'What are these arrayed in white?' The sacrament is not specifically mentioned but in it we are like the Seer with his vision of the innumerable host and their chorus of praise. We are fed at the Lord's table, but wait to see him in his glory, 'without a sacramental veil'. The wine which shows Christ's passion will soon be drunk new in 'the dazzling courts above' at the marriage supper of the Lamb. By faith and hope we are already there. 'Suffering and curse and death are o'er /and pain afflicts the soul no more'. We are 'harbour'd in the Saviour's breast', or 'safe in the arms of Jesus' as the later evangelical hymn was to say. The imagery is of tenderest intimacy (*Hymns on the Lord's Supper*, No. 93).

The extent to which the hymns influenced the devotion of ordinary Methodists is not easily assessable. Singing them would lodge them in the deep minds of worshippers, but they have hardly dominated Methodist spirituality in the years since and are little known as a eucharistic collection today, except among sacramentally inclined Methodists and scholars. In *Doxology* (1979), Geoffrey Wainwright used them to show that like creeds, hymns may be 'first-order' expressions of religious faith. They go beyond the purely rational and logical, and use figures and images which would be too daring for prose, and celebrate paradox.[6] Sacramental revival or not, by 1792 Samuel Bradburn was deploring Methodist neglect of 'the dear memorials of his dying love' [18].

---

18. Is it not enough to make us ashamed to look God in the face when we reflect upon the nature and importance of the Lord's Supper and consider how it is treated by many of the Methodists? Some are careless about it, others in a trifling spirit say they receive it as the Quakers do.

Source: S. Bradburn, *Are the Methodists Dissenters?*, Bristol 1792, cited by J. Munsey Turner, *Conflict and Reconciliation*, Epworth Press 1982, p. 27.

For discussion

1. What should be the place of the Lord's Supper in Christian Worship?

2. In what sense do you believe that the Lord's Supper is a sacrifice?

3. How do you understand the 'real Presence of Christ in the Sacrament'? Read *Hymns on the Lord's Supper*, Nos 57 and 116 (*Hymns and Psalms*, No. 629). What do they mean to you?

4. Has the sense of taste spiritual value?

5

Other Means of Grace

Fasting

The fourth means of grace is fasting. Wesley specifies Fridays. In the days of the Holy Club he had included Wednesday, the day of Christ's betrayal, as well. This was not primarily to identify with the world's hungry but as an act of penitence and, above all, of love, which denies itself for the beloved. It is better 'to abstain from pride and vanity, from foolish and hurtful desires, from peevishness and anger, and discontent than from food', but the lesser helps the greater. By fasting we shall the more easily overcome the other faults.

Association and fellowship

Fifthly, there is 'Christian conference' which means association and fellowship with other Christians. Rightly ordered conversations could minister grace. Dr Johnson said 'John Wesley's conversation is good but he is never at leisure. He is always obliged to go at a certain hour. This is very disagreeable to a man who loves to fold his legs and have his talk out as I do.' Wesley had little in common with agricultural labourers. Methodism's success with them was later and largely non-Wesleyan. He had no time for aristocrats. But he liked to be with serious, intelligent, cheerful people, interested in God and the world – the beginnings of technology for instance – and believed that much companionship was a means of grace.

Wesley also classified 'prudential' means of grace –

particular rules or acts of holy living; class and band meetings, prayer meetings, Covenant services, watchnight services, Love Feasts; visiting the sick; doing all the good one can, doing no harm; reading devotional classics and all edifying literature.

Waiting and watching

Watchnight services were thought to reproduce the vigils of the primitive church. There was among Christians a tendency to come together to await the Lord's return. The hours of darkness were particularly suggestive of the return because of the references in the Gospels to the Lord's coming as a thief in the night, or the bridegroom appearing at midnight. There was also the injunction to 'watch and pray' and the sad rebuke in Gethsemane, 'Can you not watch with me one hour?'; while the Christian use of the night for prayer was in contrast to the revels and orgies of the world which the darkness heightened.

The Covenant

The Covenant service was derived from the Puritans, Joseph and Richard Alleine – Wesley made a private custom into a congregational act, but, like the Puritans, the early Methodists also made their own private covenants with God.[1] On the other hand so did M. de Renty, and the words of the Covenant may be paralleled in the Exercises of Ignatius Loyola. The Covenant [19] is a solemn and binding pledge to devote oneself wholly to God, 'abandonment to Divine Providence'.

---

19. I am no longer my own, but thine.
Put me to what thou wilt, rank me with whom
thou wilt;
put me to doing, put me to suffering;
let me be employed for thee or laid aside for thee,
exalted for thee or brought low for thee;
let me be full, let me be empty;
let me have all things, let me have nothing;
I freely and heartily yield all things to thy pleasure
and disposal.
And now, glorious and blessed God, Father, Son
and Holy Spirit,
Thou art mine and I am thine. So be it.
And the covenant which I have made on earth,
let it be ratified in heaven.

Source: Covenant Service 1780, and subsequent editions.

The Love Feast

The Love Feast was taken over from the Moravians at Herrnhut. It looked back to the primitive a*gape*, of which some modern scholars doubt the existence, the meal of which the eucharist at first formed a part, but which became detached from it. It was a symbol of social holiness, less formal, more intimate than the sacrament. Biscuits and water were eaten and drunk and testimony given as to what God had done in believers' hearts and minds.

For discussion

1. Is the night a time of particular devotional significance? Is decline in evening worship spiritually impoverishing?

2. Discuss the biblical idea of Covenant and its importance in Christian spirituality.

3. Do the words of the Covenant 'speak to your condition'?

4. Have you experience of a Love Feast? What did it do for you?

6

Perfect Love

John Wesley attempted more seriously, say, than John Newton, to integrate various strands of Catholic spirituality into his own evangelical theology.[1] His spiritual theology was based more on 'love of God' than the 'faith in Christ' of continental and Puritan Protestantism. The Christian must aim for nothing less than perfect love, which implies sinless perfection. Otherwise the work of Christ is limited:

> Unless thou purge my every stain,
> Thy suffering and my faith are vain.[2]

It is not enough to say with Luther that 'one is always a sinner, always penitent, always justified', nor to believe with the Calvinists that the elect are given final perseverance, but are sinners to the last, albeit forgiven; the struggle is not abated and though salvation is not in doubt for the elect, their reward is governed by the extent to which they have overcome sin, or not fallen into it. The Calvinists could not sing 'I wrestle not now, but trample on sin'. God's grace would hold them to the last but the enemy was always on the offensive. Wesley claimed that Christ died not simply that we might be forgiven, but that we might be entirely sanctified. The convert, though at first a babe in Christ, must not be left without nurture or given a perpetual diet of milk, or worse still, 'cordials', sweets, with no strong meat, but encouraged, through preaching of the new law of the Sermon on the Mount, to attain to nothing less than the measure of the stature of the fullness of Christ.

This was possible. Here there were dangers. Wesley went on to claim that entry into perfection might be instantaneous, like first conversion. This doctrine not only aroused opposition on the part, for instance, of such as John Newton.[3] It led to some scandals within the Methodist Societies, extreme claims and fanatical scenes. Wesley was no more prone to be sceptical of the truth of those who said that they had reached perfection than he was of the convulsions and paroxysms which could attend his open air preaching. He insisted on a quasi-scientific investigation or survey, for he never himself claimed perfection and stood at some distance from his own movement. Ronald Knox is right when he says that while there were manifestations of enthusiasm, in the technical sense of possession by the Spirit, rather like the Toronto Blessing, all around him, 'the preacher stood there taking notes ready to publish an account of the curious manifestation in his Journal'. One of his favourite words was 'calm'.[4]

Perfection for Wesley was perfect love, the keeping of the two great commandments, and the test was whether one loved one's enemies with a heart cleansed of hatred. It was not inerrancy, nor infallibility.

Wesley may have been ignorant of the Unconscious. Was this why for him feeling was so important? 'My God, I know, I feel thee mine'? In spite of his emphasis on social holiness, he may have failed to understand sufficiently the implications of our being members one of another and that the individual cannot be perfect without a perfect society. He may have underestimated the extent and nature of sin and thought that it could be extracted like a rotten tooth, instead of being what we are, rather than a disease which infects what we do. Was he not too much of an optimist? And did not too many of his followers, and their successors, think of entry into perfection as an experience, a felt, perhaps almost frenzied excitement, rather than a moral condition evidenced by humility and a sense of the way of love still beckoning on, as with the patristic teachers we have mentioned?

Growth in grace

He did alert his followers to the necessity of growth in grace. They were not called to potter about in the foothills, but to scale the heights of holiness. And no discouragements, no fears, no cautions should deter them. The promises of scripture were there, the future imperative of Matthew 5.48, 'You shall be perfect as your Father in heaven is perfect', and those words on which Wesley's New Testament had opened on the morning of 24 May 1738, 'You should be partakers of the Divine nature' (II Peter 1.4). Wesley's insistence on the doctrine did make enemies, while some manifestations under his aegis reminded people too frighteningly of the fanatics of the years after the Civil Wars of the previous century, and seemed to mark out Methodists as sectarians of the most dangerous kind. Yet Wesley's teaching does have affinities with Catholic and Orthodox spirituality, especially as it was turned into hymns like this:

> Since the Son has made me free,
> Let me taste my liberty,

> Thee behold with open face,
> Triumph in thy saving grace,
> Thy great will delight to prove,
> Glory in thy perfect love.[5]

The verses which follow, addressed severally to each person of the Trinity, are very bold in asking for all promises to be fulfilled, all grace to be showered upon the suppliant, 'all the joy and peace and power ... all the life and heaven of love' so that it be no longer I but Christ living in the flesh. A. M. Allchin has compared this with the teaching of the Byzantine saint of the eleventh century, Symeon, the New Theologian. 'He, too, taught with a similar emphasis that Christians of every age are expected to know and to feel all that the first Christians knew and felt, that there is no diminution in the action of the Spirit throughout the ages.'[6]

For discussion

1. Are perfectionists unpleasant people?

2. Bearing in mind the confusions and ambiguities that surround the idea of 'love', what are the qualities of 'perfect love'?

3. What is the connection between love and the gift of the Spirit?

7

The Social Gospel

21. The Spirit of the Lord is upon me, because he hath anointed me to preach the Gospel to the poor; he hath sent me to heal the broken-hearted, to preach deliverance to the captives, and recovering of sight to the blind, to set at liberty them that are bruised, to preach the acceptable year of the Lord.

Source: Luke 4.16.

R. W. Dale, the nineteenth-century Birmingham Congregationalist theologian, claimed that the doctrine of Christian perfection should make Methodists social reformers.[1] Wesley cannot be claimed as such – he never mentions the harsh poor laws, or inveighs against the barbarity of capital punishment for minor offences – and he had little faith in political action. He was a Tory who, had he known it, could never have embraced Socialism. This may be thought inconsistent, for Socialism is perfectionism, and there have been many Methodist Socialists, witness their influence on the working-class movements and the Labour Party in its origins. Wesley's concern for the poor is, however, constant.[2] With de Renty, he saw their rags as 'purpled over with the blood of Christ'. He chose Luke 4.16 as the text of his first open-air sermon [21]. His fidelity to the Christ of the Synoptic Gospels would make him feel that the poor were nearer to the kingdom than the rich:

In most genteel religious people there is so strange a mixture that I have seldom much confidence in them. I love the poor; in many of them I find pure, serious grace, unmixed with paint, folly and affectation.

And again: 'If I might choose, I would still (as I have done hitherto) preach the gospel to the poor.'

Faith and works

He may have romanticized the poor. The itinerant did not have to live among the same poor for years on end, and he may have ignored their crimes. But this mission to the poor combined faith and works, care for their bodies as well as souls and is an instance at once of his New Testament Christianity and his love of people, of our pitiful yet enthralling humanity.

There was a suggestion by the Conference of 1748 that rich people should have a longer period as members on trial than the poor. Methodist chapels did not, as in Lady Huntingdon's Connexion, at this stage have rented pews for the wealthier. In spite of his famous sermon on 'The Use of Money' – 'Gain all you can; Save all you can; Give all you can' – Wesley did not think that Christians should covet or amass riches. In 1744, he had some thought of reviving in the Societies the 'Christian communism' of the Acts of the Apostles. The discipline he practised was not simply an ascetic attempt to save his soul, but in order that he might give to the poor, which he did generously. Throughout his life he was not ashamed to beg for them, as he did as an old man in his eighties in the London snow. The poor evoked all the tenderness of his nature. He had memories of the financial struggles in the Rectory at Epworth, as well as of his Oxford penury, and philanthropy in days which in some moods he thought were the best of his life. He abominated patronage. Charity should preserve the dignity of the poor and should not be remote and impersonal, but the means of forming relationships. 'How much better it is, when it can be done, to carry relief to the poor, rather than to send it.'

---

22.   Jesus, the gift divine I know,
      The gift divine I ask of thee;
      That living water now bestow,
      Thy Spirit and thyself on me.
Thou, Lord, of life the fountain art,
Now let me find thee in my heart!

      Thee let me drink and thirst no more
      For drops of finite happiness;
      Spring up, O well, in heavenly power,
      In springs of pure perennial peace,
In peace which none can take away,
In joy which shall for ever stay.

      Father on me the grace bestow.
      Unblameable before thy sight,
      Whence all the streams of mercy flow;
      Mercy, thy own supreme delight
To me, for Jesu's sake impart,
And plant thy nature in my heart.

      Thy mind throughout my life be shown
      While listening to the wretch's cry
      The widow's and the orphan's groan,
      On mercy's wings I swiftly fly
The poor and helpless to relieve
My life, my all, for them to give.

      Thus may I show the Spirit within,
      Which purges me from every stain,
      Unspotted from the world and sin
      My faith's integrity maintain.
The truth of my religion prove
By perfect purity and love.

Source: 1780 *Collection*, No. 7.

Franz Hildebrandt and others have thought that authentic Methodist spirituality is contained in a paraphrase of Psalm 123 [22]. Not all have found Methodist devotion admirable in practice. Some have seen it as grim, joyless, and 'Philistine', hostile to the arts, perverting all that was healthy in human emotions. One of Wesley's preachers, John Pawson, burnt Wesley's copy of Shakespeare with its copious notes as 'worthless lumber, not tending to edification'.[3] Many of the preachers after his death inherited something of his ecumenical spirituality – the *Christian Library* sold better in the nineteenth century than when it was first published – but not his love of literature.

Criticisms include the fact that some forms of Methodism led to political reaction and smothered the growth of working-class consciousness. The class-meeting led to an introspection which diverted the members from the need to improve social conditions, while 'espionage into each other's moral failings was encouraged'.[4] The immensely influential work by E. P. Thompson, son of a Methodist minister, on *The Making of the English Working Class* has not commended Methodism. We may concede that, as in all religious and human institutions, the good may be perverted, though Thompson goes on to unwarranted and exaggerated extremes.[5] There was, though, the driving of 'a dangerous wedge between the sacred and the secular if the idea is to be pursued that the world is to be used, while God is to be enjoyed'.[6] These tensions would continue for the rest of Methodist history until our own time.

For discussion

1. Does politics have anything to do with religion?

2. How do we care for the poor?

3. What is the relation between God and the world? Is 'worldliness' the enemy of the Christian life?

PART II

NINETEENTH-CENTURY DEVELOPMENTS

8

Communion with God

The scantiest survey of Methodism in the nineteenth century makes us aware that many of the distinctive characteristics of the earliest days remained, and that Wesley himself exercised remarkable posthumous influence in governing the devotional habits and the spiritual reading of his people for many generations.

Thomas Collins

What would Lopez and de Renty have thought had they known that their immortality would rest not simply on the fashionable salons of Paris or the parsonages of rural England, but on the diary references of broad-backed, stentorian, travelling preachers of the lower-middle classes who laboured in the grime of an industrial civilization they could never have conceived? There was, for instance, a Wesleyan minister named Thomas Collins, who lived from 1810 to 1864, worked with intense evangelical ardour in many circuits from Orkney to Camborne, and not only read Lopez and de Renty but experienced something of their immediacy of communion with God. As a young minister in his twenties at Sandhurst, Collins wrote: 'I do in some measure give myself unto prayer; but O that I could feel that experience of Gregory Lopez mine: Every breath is prayer!'[1] When he was dying, he devised a new almanack of devotion based on the three Persons of the Trinity, of whom, according to his biography, he had long, like the Marquis de Renty, carried about 'an experimental verity'.[2]

When he was asked about this, he replied:

I am in possession of no secret. I have never either looked for, or had, anything mystical, beyond what plain Scriptures warrant. I do not suppose that I have any divine manifestations peculiar to myself. The ordering of my thoughts in the manner I have told you of is not 'of commandment' – is not the result of any extraordinary leading. It began as a mental choice; being found convenient and profitable, it has grown into a habit. In acts of devotion my mind sees its way most clearly when it talks with one Person. I, therefore, seeking edification, speak unto each of the ever-glorious Three distinctly in behalf of such things, and such things only, as Holy Scripture sets forth to be the province of each distinctly.[3]

In the prayer of Collins' last days, which follows, the three Persons are addressed in turn, the Father as Strength and Joy, ever-beloved, to be glorified in death; the Son as the One who of old led his people through the Red Sea and will bear Collins safe through the waves of his departure from this world; the Spirit as the gift of Jesus, living and active in response to faith; the Triune God as omniscient Helper to whose will the soul must be resigned. There is some danger of tritheism here, since Christian prayer is *to* the Father, *through* Son, *in* the Holy Spirit, and the doctrine of the Trinity, vital to Christian Faith, is of personality *in* God rather than the personality *of* God.

Collins disclaimed 'mystical' experience, which he seems to regard as reserved for the spiritual aristocracy and dubiously scriptural. Yet more than once this man, who would sometimes spend Friday in 'secret fasting, meditation, and prayer for help on the Lord's Day', knew an immediacy of the Divine Presence, which has some of the marks of classical mysticism. On the Covenant Sunday of 1849, for instance, as, about five o'clock in the morning, he was preparing for the solemnities of the renewal:

> I was waiting upon God in believing acts. He mercifully drew near to me, as once – only once before – He did years ago, on the Rock of Skarfskerry. His coming darkened and distanced all earthly things. My soul felt as if within the cloud of Tabor. While it hung around me, I cried, 'I know Thee! Yes I know Thee!' The ineffable glory did not long abide, such specialities of manifestation never do; but in its gentle ascent it left a sweet life, a calm, a tenderness which cannot be expressed.[4]

The darkness and the cloud, the ineffable glory, and the transcendency of the experience are typical of that Augustinian and Western Mysticism described by Abbot Cuthbert Butler.[5]

On Christmas Day 1864, two days before his death, Collins repeated lines from Charles Wesley's hymn on the Crucified – 'With glorious clouds encompassed round' [23]. He died trusting in the blood of Jesus and healed by the stripes of the smitten Shepherd. He had always preached the Atoning

---

23. Will He forsake His throne above.
    Himself to worms impart?
    Answer thou man of Grief and Love!
    And speak it to my heart.

    Source: 1780 *Collection*, No. 124.

Sacrifice. It was Thomas Collins who when a Cornish butcher of wicked life cried out in agony of conscience 'I am lost! I am lost! I have nothing!' replied, 'Nothing? Why, man, *all the hill of Calvary belongs to you.*'[6]

William Clowes

There is no more remarkable instance in nineteenth-century Methodism of the prayer of communion with God than that imparted by the Primitive Methodist preacher John Nelson in his reminiscences of William Clowes (1780-1851), co-founder of his Connexion. Clowes, be it noted, had undergone a disturbance of the spirit prior to conversion when he recalled at a Methodist Love Feast a phrase from the Book of Common Prayer about taking the sacrament unworthily, so that the Anglican divines were his spiritual ancestors as truly as they were those of Methodism as a whole. But it was not echoes of the Prayer Book which impressed those who said of him, 'We never heard prayer like this ... He lived and moved as though he were on the borders of the heavenly world.' During long and arduous missions in the north, he would every now and then ask for an hour in which to pour out his soul to God, and he would do so without any agony, conflict, or wrestling [24].

---

24. Sometimes when sojourning in the home of pious poverty, where there was not a second room where he could enter, he would say to the good woman of the house: 'Now I want to pray; pursue thy work: never mind me.' And then without a word he would quietly kneel down in the most retired corner, where he could remain for an hour. Generally there was no audible expression ... no sound heard ... There was an awful stillness ... He somehow in his solemn quiet sweetly sank into God, till he became motionless as a statue.

Source: John Nelson, verbal reminiscences of Clowes, cited in J. T. Wilkinson, *William Clowes*, Epworth Press 1951, pp. 85–86.

Sacrifice of the missionaries

The nineteenth-century missionaries, sent out by all branches of the by now fissiparous Methodism, testify in their journals to many experiences of immediate encounter with God, though perhaps the language of devotion becomes rather conventional. [I] 'was enabled last night to enter "the holiest of all" and hold communion sweet and rapturous with God' is a not untypical entry from a missionary's diary. There is much about 'the secret place', a phrase which in these days causes a snigger. Yet these men went out to the African fields in the knowledge that the climate and conditions might kill them in months if not weeks. The toll of lives was appalling and those who remained were victims of almost incessant fevers.[7] They were in many respects 'massively heroic', counting all things loss for Christ. They do not seem to have had any doubts as to the truth of the gospel they offered, and they died, often triumphantly, with Wesley's hymns on their lips, sure that they would be 'forever with the Lord'. They knew that they were supported by the Societies at home. No account of Methodist devotion is complete without some reference to the great interest in missions overseas and the prayer which has sustained them. They knew also that behind their sacrificial efforts was the support of British civil and military power. But this did not deliver them from many hazards, and their secret is disclosed in the story of James Calvert, missionary to the cannibals in Fiji who, once asked by a timid listener when he was on furlough 'Were you not afraid of being killed?' replied 'No, we died before we went.'[8]

In the late 1930s, Dietrich Bonhoeffer held up the example of these missionaries to the pastors of the Confessional Church in Nazi Germany:

I am not asking you to do or suffer anything new. This has always been the way of the witness. What, over there in Richmond College, there are boards with the names of the Methodist missionaries who died on the field and when one fell there was another to take his place.[9]

The heroism was not confined to the Wesleyans. The United Methodist Free Churches could tell similar stories of their missionaries to Africa and China. All branches of Methodism had their overseas witnesses.

Modern political correctness reduces them to agents of British imperialism. They believed that they were offering Christian civilization as well as eternal salvation in Christ. We must not judge them by the standards and realisms of another age. Their heroic, sacrificial love for Christ is of the perennial dimension of Christian spirituality.

For discussion

1. Is the doctrine of the Trinity a help to your prayers?

2. Are there people such as William Clowes and James Calvert in the church today? If not, why not?

3. Have you had an experience like that of Thomas Collins at Skarfskerry or on Covenant Sunday 1849? If so, what have been its consequences?

4. Were the sacrificial missionaries ambassadors not so much of Christ, as they thought, but of British imperialism?

9

The Developing Church Consciousness

Though it was an age of world-wide expansion and great triumphs, the nineteenth century confronted Methodism with all the problems of continuing existence in the world; and, most notably, how to establish a durable church order and how to adapt itself to social changes. Some of the problems were direct bequests from John Wesley himself. His widespread sowing sprouted a harvest of ambiguities and controversies as well as heroism, spirituality and intense faith.

Relations with the established church

For much of the century, Methodism lived in a love-hate relationship with the established church. It is difficult not to feel that Methodism ought to have had such an effect upon the Church of England as to make the later Oxford Movement unnecessary. Why it failed is a very complex matter; one very clear reason is that after the Holy Club it had little or no influence in the universities, and – snobbish as it sounds – movements of reform cannot succeed without capturing the intelligentsia to a greater extent than Methodism has ever done, at least in England. (Its part in helping to create a West Indian, African and American intelligentsia is another story.) But there is a particular irony in the fact that, as has several times been pointed out, it was early Methodist loyalty to the Church of England, which at once destroyed the leavening power it might have had and seriously impoverished its own spiritual life.[1] Had

not the Plan of Pacification (1795) been so anxious to avoid the appearance of rivalry to the established church and refused to permit the celebration of the Lord's Supper at church hours, the crowded communions of the Wesleys, which made the revival sacramental as well as evangelical, might have been a feature of Methodism to the present day and made the Societies heralds of the liturgical movement.

A distinct sacramentalism

At the same time, it must be recognized that this judgment could be over-sanguine. The sacramentalism of the Methodist people in its heyday was different from that of the Catholic tradition – and the Puritan – and we must not allow our own quiet devotional reading of the hymns on the Lord's Supper to mislead us into a false idea of the atmosphere of eighteenth-century Methodist communion services. They were gospel feasts rather than holy mysteries, and the belief that the Supper was a 'converting ordinance' was a departure from the whole of Christian tradition even though *evangelical* conversion is implied, rather than a first turning from sin to God.

It must not be thought that the sacraments meant nothing to nineteenth-century saints. Luke Tyerman told the story of *Praying William*.[2] This old man had a very serious attitude to baptism, and his minister described a communion service at which William was present. William began, as his custom was, to shout God's praises, but his voice faltered and his body shook. A sense of most sacred and solemn power filled the chapel. The minister looked at William, 'his countenance lit up with joy and his body literally trembling', and thought of the words:

> He visits now His house of clay
> He shakes His future home.

The congregation rose, but William, 'unconscious of any presence save that of Christ still kept kneeling and praising God'.

This is intense and genuine sacramental devotion but its differences from the Catholic tradition are perhaps as important as its similarities. Here is much more noise and 'enthusiasm', more obvious working up and psychological release. Christ possesses William rather than the bread and wine, which are not so much as mentioned; indeed the real presence is subjective rather than objective. 'The most sacred and solemn power' is in direct consequence of what happens to William, not to the eucharistic species. William might, through a common love of Jesus, have understood the Breton peasant who, when he was asked why he spent so many hours on his knees before the reserved sacrament replied, 'I look at Him; He looks at me.' But he would not have been at home with the visual images or been able to direct his contemplation to the sacrament itself. The darkened church, heavy with incense and *pieta*, could not have been the context of William's inspiration. He needed the bare chapel, probably bright in comparison, his fellow members of society around him, and the custom of vocal, noisy prayer.

From another branch of Methodism, Dr Beckerlegge, in an article of 1964, described the evening communion services of his youth, twentieth-century in fact, but carried over from the nineteenth.[3] This is typical of most nineteenth-century practice. And before we deplore it as an impoverishment of what was or might have been, it is well to recognize that it represented a genuine intended fidelity to Christ's command and had a distinctive power, albeit different from Catholic sacramentalism.

Increasing differences

Certainly the differences from the Church of England began to be increasingly emphasized as the century wore on. The Oxford Movement despised and deplored Methodism, though some of its successors tried to recover the eucharistic hymns.[4] But Pusey, although acknowledging the reality of Methodist conversions, called theirs 'a naked gospel' denuded of the sacramental robes of the apostolic order which clothes and protects and graces the soul. Methodists feared the Catholicizing tendencies of the Oxford fathers. The very mention of 'Puseyism' would throw the Wesleyan Conference into howls of rage and it was rumoured that Methodist parents subdued recalcitrant offspring with the threat 'Be good, or Dr Pusey'll get you!'[5] A redoubtable Methodist theologian, Dr J. H. Rigg, disliked Anglicanism as a whole, in his youth attacked the theology of F. D. Maurice, regarded Anglicanism as insignificant in comparison with world-wide Methodism and deplored 'that system of theurgic mysticism which our modern High Anglicans have substituted for the glorious gospel of the Blessed God' . The 1904 Methodist hymnbook amends the fourth verse of Henry Francis Lyte's 'Praise, my soul, the King of Heaven' to avoid the invocation of angels, and changes 'Son of Mary' to 'Son of David' in Henry Hart Milman's funeral hymn 'When our heads are bowed with woe'.

There is a difference of mood as well as of style. 'Holiness rather than peace' was Newman's slogan, though he learned it from his evangelical mentor, Thomas Scott. It contrasts with Wesley's 'Holiness is happiness' , though the contrast here may be of Calvinism and Arminianism and it could be argued that Wesley's sentiments are the more Catholic. In spite of bitterness and controversy there was a deeper kinship beneath the surface than appeared from the outside. There was no point of contact to make understanding possible.[6]

Even before the Oxford Movement, there were signs of a weakening of those Church of England ties which in some ways had bound Wesley himself even more strongly after 1738. Thomas Jackson's edition of Wesley's works is comprehensive enough but, for some unaccountable reason, he omitted the Homilies of the Church of England, which Wesley published at the very time when he discovered in his own experience the meaning of justification by faith alone.

There remained in Methodism a great love for the Book of Common Prayer. Adam Clarke would have no truck with Wesley's abridgement.[7] When the non-Wesleyan bodies began to devise their own service books because there were 'certain special and solemn occasions which ought not to be left to the discretion of ministers or other presiding brethren', they neither wished nor were able to break free of its hallowed forms. Some Methodists have read the daily Psalms in private and family devotion. But there has also been suspicion and dislike. The Islington Circuit sent a memorial to the Wesleyan Conference in 1874, urging that 'a revised and safe liturgy should be prepared and used instead of the Book of Common Prayer'. But this was after relations had deteriorated post-Oxford Movement, as was the complaint against the headmaster of a Wesleyan day-school in the Midlands, who used each morning in assembly, the third collect for grace, 'O Lord and heavenly Father, Almighty and Everlasting God, who hast safely brought us to the beginning of this day . . .'

Nineteenth-century Methodists may have differed in their use of Wesley's forms or in the tradition of ordered diurnal piety. There was, however, a continual admiration of holiness wherever it was found. A Methodist preacher could write thus of the Jesuit founders, Ignatius Loyola and Francis Xavier: ' If the generality of that order have been deemed the most insidious of men, I think it equitable to avow my opinion that the founders of this institution were persons of deepest piety.'[8]

Controversies and ambiguities

The violent and bitter controversies within nineteenth-century Methodism were all the result of attempts to resolve the ambiguities of Wesley's legacy. They were about government, not spirituality. The authority of the ministers was the nub of the contentions, but the issue concerned political power and central government rather than the lordship of faith, although there continued among the Wesleyans an antipathy towards lay administration of the sacraments, which caused a strong party to oppose Methodist union in the 1920s.[9] It was ministerial rule which the non-Wesleyans so resented, for this was not the tyranny of a parish priest, powerful only within the limits of a defined area and checked by the existence of a slow moving, not very efficient hierarchy. It was the claim by an exclusively ministerial conference to legislate for every society in the kingdom. The nineteenth century saw Methodism creaking and groaning into democracy, the non-Wesleyans by violent schism, the Wesleyans by gradual evolution.

It is easy to say that the separated and rival Methodists preached the same gospel, sang the same hymns and prayed with the same fervour, but internecine controversy cannot be good for a company of Christians who claim perfect love as their grand depositum, and who inherit the sermon on the *Catholic Spirit*. But, apart from this, the whole transition from Societies to church clearly resulted in the slackening of discipline, for while a Society, like a religious order, consists of people of like minds, pledged to a rule of life, who may leave or be dismissed if they do not wish to obey, a church is inevitably a mixed body or, if you like, a dragnet which will bring in a curious and varied haul.

Throughout the nineteenth century, Methodism became increasingly unhappy about its failure to help its converts to grow in the Christian life. It has been said, apropos the Bible Christians, that both they and the Wesleyan Methodists, who spread side by side throughout north Devon in the fifty years after Waterloo, differed from the Prayer Book because they asserted that a personal Christian experience rather than baptism was the essential 'precondition of anything which can properly be called a Christian life'.[10]

But the records of Methodist history raise the

question whether such personal experience is any more effective in ensuring that the believer endures to the end or, less dramatically, makes real progress in the school of Christian love.

Numerous tracts were published urging the revival of real religion and the pressing on towards holiness. But in spite of the intensity of the few there is little doubt that the many were always in danger of growing cold. Samuel Coley, a theological tutor at Headingley College, was forced to conclude: 'Methodism has done much and well by *conquest* but only little and inadequately by *nurture*.'[11]

For discussion

1. If possible read the 1937 Methodist Report on 'The Nature of the Christian Church'. Does this vindicate Methodism's emerging from a revival and an order to a church with the same essential characteristics as other denominations?

2. 'How these Christians hate one another?' Why is this still more evident in sectarian conflicts than love? What is its cure?

3. Should Methodism have remained an 'order' within the Church of England and not acquired the organization of a church? Would this have been possible?

10

Revivalism

In all this we may detect a shift of emphasis. It may be argued that throughout the nineteenth century and until the union of 1932, there was a crisis of identity in Methodism which produced a two-fold tension. From 1795 there was no chance of Methodism becoming a religious order within the Anglican communion (though the latter phrase is an anachronism). The question was 'Is Methodism a church and if so what kind of a church?', but in addition there was a haunting, half-embarrassed, half-conscience-stricken murmur, 'Is Methodism a church or a series of revivals'? The High Wesleyans, of whom Jabez Bunting was the much maligned representative leader, deplored the alternative, and were made uneasy by revivalists, whom they regarded as undisciplined and divisive.

There has been, and still is, a school of Christian thought which would seem to regard Christianity as existing in this imperfect world by a dialectical process of revival – decline – revival. The gospel is preached, many respond, but in time their religion becomes formal and lifeless, and so there is need for a new Pentecost [25].

In many Methodist Circuits and Societies of the nineteenth century, it seems to have been assumed that revival would be necessary every few years. The phrase 'Hedgerow religion' was used in Cornwall where there were constant revivals. A week's 'mission' became a feature of Methodist life, and although the hope was that this way local profligates and unbelievers would be brought in and converted (as indeed happened), there is little doubt that the main purpose of the preaching was to fan the flame

25. For several years, some of our members in different societies have appeared remarkably zealous in public worship, and have shown a disposition to assume the name of *Revivalists*; but a wish to preserve the union of the body induced us to check, with constant care, every distinction that in the least tended to a party spirit.

Source: T. P. Bunting, *Life of Bunting*, Appendix K, quoted by H. B. Kendal in *A New History of Methodism*, I, 1909, p. 556.

within the lukewarm society. Of course, such missions were not the monopoly of Methodists or evangelicals in the nineteenth century. They were a feature of Anglo- and Roman Catholic church life, though there, the emphasis may have been more exclusively on Calvary and less on Pentecost.

The greatest and most permanent revival within Methodism was that in the first decade of the century which began in those parts of north Staffordshire and south-east Cheshire dominated by the 'bleak and frowning summit' of Mow Cop. This is particularly relevant to our subject since it was so closely associated with prayer.

The 'prayer meeting' was not a very common title in the eighteenth century, though John Wesley occasionally spoke with approval of it, and it is obvious that the bands and classes gave opportunities for free and spontaneous outpourings by members. Particularly was this so in the 'cottage meetings' which by the end of the century had become characteristic of Methodist life in some regions of north-west industrial England. In north Staffordshire, these cottage meetings, though 'lively and loud', were kept under strict control and limited to an hour and a half in time. This annoyed some who were denied the chance to express themselves in prayer and to these Daniel Shubotham, the cousin whom Hugh Bourne had converted, promised 'a whole day's praying on Mow some Sunday'.

Influence of the camp meetings

It was not, however, until Bourne and his friends, who were already exercising an irregular revivalist ministry in the Potteries and north Staffordshire coal fields, were introduced to the strolling American evangelist, Lorenzo Dow, that the promise was fulfilled. Dow told them of the camp meetings which had begun in America at the beginning of the century and were part of the technique of revivalism which was winning remarkable victories on the 'frontier'.[1] They were not confined to Methodism, but Asbury commended and encouraged them. They were, as a rule, typical scenes of religious enthusiasm, not without its attendant dangers. It is in some ways incongruous to think of the hymns of Isaac Watts, if not of the more rapturous Charles Wesley, being used to rouse their fervour; though as time went on, less poetic ditties were sung. At the Cane Ridge revival in Kentucky in 1801, Presbyterians, Baptists and Methodists were joined. The weekend of 6 August began normally enough, but by the Sunday there was an atmosphere of unearthly joy and many were 'convicted of sin'. One account noted that 'they say they feel very weak in their knees and a want of breath ...' Ministers would then have the stricken carried out of the crowd and would converse, pray and exhort each one. Others might sing an appropriate hymn. After a lapse of time the person might 'get comfort' through divine release and would exclaim, 'Lord have mercy', then proceed to exhortations that onlookers cease doing evil, depend on Christ's righteousness, and in their turn seek the Lord ... Later stages were less restrained. Formal sermons seemed to give way, at least in part, to small prayer circles of ten or twelve, each of which would sing a different Watts hymn, to be interrupted by a preacher mounting a stump or log to begin an informal discourse or fervent exhortation. One young man who attended later recalled that 'the noise was like the roar of Niagara', the people 'agitated as if by a storm'. He soon felt a peculiarly strange sensation ... 'My heart beat tumultuously, my knees trembled, my lip quivered, and I felt as though I must fall to the ground.' Fleeing to the woods, he returned to have the same experience again. 'My hair rose up on my head, my whole frame trembled, the blood ran cold in my veins, and I fled for the woods a second time, and wished I had staid at home.' Feeling almost suffocated and blind, he felt he would die; after a dismal night among the trees he set out for home, experiencing conversion the next day.[2]

The Methodists in England were suspicious of such uncontrolled excitement which, so it was darkly hinted, fell easily into sensual excess; they had also been warned against Lorenzo Dow by an American leader who disapproved of his inveterate freelancing and considered him a charlatan.[3] But Bourne, Clowes and Shubotham immediately saw that the camp meeting could be an outlet and extension of the enthusiasm which was engulfing the Societies within the shadow of Mow. They also realized that held at the Wakes time, these assemblies could counteract the evils of the fairs.

There was a difference between those camp meetings, which were organs of the Primitive Methodist Connexion, and their American prototypes. In a sense, the former were not camp meetings, for each lasted but a day, albeit a long one. This, of itself, would be a safeguard against certain obvious perils.

Meetings on Mow Cop

At the first camp meeting on Mow Cop there were four preaching stands constructed for the occasion out of pieces of rock, and each offer of the gospel was supported by praying companies on other parts of the hill and beneath the wagonettes. Fervour, intensity and noise there was and singing of Wesley hymns, but not the extremes of Cane Ridge. Indeed, Bourne seems to have been most impressed with the sight of 'thousands hearing with attention solemn as death', and modern writers of the Primitive Methodist tradition have stressed the centrality of prayer and the retreat to Mow Cop in order 'to seek comparative seclusion for a prolonged approach to God'.[4] And so, in time, a further Methodist Connexion was born. But our concern is not simply with the fervent, revivalist prayer of the camp meetings, but also with the manifestation of a lay spirituality, spontaneous, of the people, and without sex distinction, which makes inevitable a comparison between Primitive Methodism and early Quakerism.

It was hardly to be expected that so acute a scholar as Dr G. F. Nuttall would read J. T. Wilkinson's biographies *Hugh Bourne* and *William Clowes*[5] without being stimulated to essay such a comparison.[6] Hugh Bourne had read Quaker books before his conversion and his desire for open-air worship was not derived from Lorenzo Dow so much as from the writings of the first Quakers. He visited the 'Quaker Methodists' of Warrington, whose cottage meetings – detached and indeed outlawed by the Wesleyan Connexion – may well have been the inspiration of those with which he was connected in north Staffordshire. 'Here each one does that which is right in his own eyes. They stand, sit, kneel, pray, exhort, etc., as they are moved. I was very fond of their way.'[7] In their turn, some of the Quaker Methodists attended the camp meetings on Mow Cop and Norton-le-Moors.

Affinities with early Quakerism

That Primitive Methodism did not find its spiritual home in union with the Society of Friends may be due to the fact that it was early rather than contemporary Quakerism with which Bourne had such affinities. By 1807, the Quakers were for the most part a different social group from the industrial men and women along the course of the Trent whom the

Primitive Methodists influenced. Again Primitive Methodism (though this may be exaggerated) was something of a mass movement, which nineteenth-century Quakerism was not.

In *The Holy Spirit in Puritan Faith and Experience*, Dr Nuttall mentions two opposing views as to the relationship of Quakerism to Protestantism and Puritanism. Was it 'the fag-end of the Reformation' or 'true Puritanism, purged of extraneous elements and carried to a conclusion not only logical but desirable'?[8] The same question may be raised about Primitive Methodism and its parent body; but it is not wise to stay for an answer, for we are dealing not with logic but with revivals, the movements of the human spirit which cannot be categorized and classified like butterflies in cases. All the same, there were very few, after the first excitement was over, who passed from Wesleyan to Primitive Methodism as to the logical end of their religious experience. Throughout the nineteenth century in all branches of Methodism there was a perennial longing for revival, revival, and still more revival. On 9 September 1848, Thomas Collins' father wrote to his son:

> The present slow advance of Methodism becomes a grief to me. Surely our array – ministers, local preachers, leaders, prayer leaders, sick visitors, tract distributors, teachers – ought to accomplish greater things. O for a baptism of the Holy Ghost! Bethesda was troubled before it could cure; and we must be better to do more. When fire infuseth its vehement heat, water seems all alive with motion. So when power from God thrills a Church, members and officers are full of holy zeal, penitents move, and the neighbourhood is stirred.[9]

William Arthur's *The Tongue of Fire*

The manual which epitomized this longing and aided its satisfaction was William Arthur's *The Tongue of Fire or the True Power of Christianity* first published in 1856. This went through eighteen impressions in its first three years, and was still regarded as of sufficient importance to warrant a centenary edition in 1956.

Arthur was an Irishman whose life, from 1819 to 1901, was almost coterminous with that of Queen Victoria. He was loaned to the Wesleyan Missionary Society by the Irish Conference and had a short spell in Mysore, curtailed by an infection of the eyes. On his return, he was for most of his ministry a secretary of the Missionary Society, but he also served in several London circuits, as Principal of the Methodist College at Belfast, and as President of the Conference. A serious weakness of the throat limited his preaching activities, but *The Tongue of Fire* is said to have begun as a sermon, which met with a similar reception to the famous lengthy utterance of the old Cambridge Puritan, Lawrence Chadderton, who when he would have finished, was bidden 'For God's sake, Sir, go on! Go on!'

Arthur's book is a study of Pentecost, which,

though preserving a literalness and a historicity quite out of fashion today, is full of psychological understanding, keen imagination and apt analogy. He has the gift of entering closely into the hearts and minds of the followers of Jesus as they waited for Pentecost. How long the days after the Ascension must have seemed! Was the promise, after all, in vain? Whatever their distress and doubt they waited, and (contrary to the besetting sin of revivalists and evangelists as Arthur knew it) they did not reproach one another, or probe too deeply into the cause of the delay by tortuous self-examination [26].

Indeed, Arthur's book is as clearly a corrective to the dangers of revivalism as it is a positive plea for hearts open to the power of the Holy Spirit. His Irish

---

26. John does not turn upon Peter and say, 'It is your fault; for you denied the Master.' Philip does not turn to John and say, 'It is your fault; for you and James wanted to lord it over us all.' Andrew does not turn to Thomas and say, 'It is your fault; for you *would* not believe, even when we had declared it to you.' The Seventy do not say, 'It is the fault of the twelve; for, after the Lord had lifted them above us all, one of them sold Him, another denied Him, and a third disbelieved.' The Marys do not say, 'It is the fault of the whole company, a cold and unfaithful company, professing to love the Master to His face, but the moment He fell into the hands of His enemies, ye all forsook Him and fled?'...

Yet they knew He had not come to call the righteous but sinners, to repentance ... He knew every fault with which any of them could charge the others; yet the promise which had passed His lips, and the fire would fall on them unworthy as they were. Happy for them that none felt that he could fix on others the cause of their unanswered prayers.

Source: William Arthur, *The Tongue of Fire*, London 1856, pp. 18–19.

---

27. Against such forms, suitably mingled with the prayer of the Church, we mean to say no word; we use, admire and enjoy them; but with the Acts of the Apostles open, it is impossible to repress astonishment that any man should imagine that frequent and formal reading of the best forms ever written, unmixed even by one outburst of spontaneous supplication from minister or people has any pretence to be looked on as the interceding grace, the gift of supplication bestowed upon the primitive Church ... That in such modes holy and prayerful hearts may and do pour themselves out to God, we not only concede but would maintain against all who questioned it. That such prayers are in many ways preferable to the one set prayer of one dry man – long, stiff and meagre – wherewith congregations are often visited, is too plain to need acknowledgment.

But gifts of prayer are part of the work and prerogative of the Holy Ghost ... In no form is the tongue of fire more impressive, more calculated to convince men that a power above nature is working, when poor men, who could no more preach than they could fly, and could not suitably frame a paragraph on any secular topic, lift up a reverent voice amid a few fellow Christians, and in strains of earnest trust, perhaps of glorious emotion, and even of sublime conception as to things Divine, plead in prayer with their Redeemer.

Source: William Arthur, *The Tongue of Fire*, London 1856, p. 90.

Protestant upbringing had given him an implacable hatred of Jesuistry, nor could he be expected to feel any tolerance towards Rome in the days of Pope Pius IX, who was later to preside over the First Vatican Council which proclaimed papal infallibility. But he is clearly a man of evangelical mean in the controversy about set forms and extempore prayers, even though he insists that the pentecostal gift is of spontaneous, unfettered prayer of the heart [27].[10]

Arthur will not have it that the Pentecostal gift is the same as the glossolalia 'speaking with tongues' of I Corinthians 14 and other passages: it is rather a sign of 'a message from the Father of men to *all* men'. Thus he implicitly rebukes the extremists. Later, he declares that this is not one of the permanent gifts of Pentecost. Neither does he ignore the sacraments [28].

William Arthur believes as strongly as Wesley that Christianity is a social religion, in two senses. The church is the society of those who are each other's guides, philosophers and friends in the Christian life. He would probably have subscribed to the belief that outside the church there is no salvation, provided it were understood that the church is not primarily a hierarchic order, handed down from the first days, a supernatural aura surrounding its priests and rites: it is the fellowship of committed believers, 'who kindly help each other on'. Nothing shows a more lamentable misunderstanding of evangelical Christianity than Father Hubert Northcott's assertion that 'John Bunyan's Christian had to leave home and kindred and set out on a lonely path. Here and there a companion joined him, but his pilgrimage remained a terribly solitary affair till he got to its end beyond the river.'[11]

William Arthur is nearer the truth: 'Banish from the Pilgrim's progress the social element, the fellowship of hearts, the free recital of the Lord's dealings with each pilgrim, and you would cool its interest down to a point which, doubtless, would be decorous in the eyes of some, but would never touch the many.'[12]

Arthur also knows that Pentecost points to the 'general renewal of society' [29]. He is very much aware of the evils of society, but he has also stumbled on the paradox so powerfully expressed in our century by Reinhold Niebuhr – 'moral man and immoral society'. 'Fearful social evils may coexist with a state of society wherein many are holy, and all have a large amount of Christian light.'[13]

---

29. The most dangerous perversion of the Gospel, viewed as affecting individuals, is, when it is looked upon as a salvation for the soul after it leaves the body, but no salvation from sin while here. The most dangerous perversion of it viewed as affecting the community, is when it is looked upon as a means of forming a holy community in the world to come but never in this.

Source: William Arthur, *The Tongue of Fire*, London 1856, p. 87.

---

28. On the day of Pentecost Christianity faced the world, a new religion and a poor one, without a history, without a priesthood, without a college, without a people and without a patron. She had only her two sacraments and her tongue of fire.

They continued steadfast 'in breaking of bread'; hence it is plain that it is not a purely spiritual system of worship, too spiritual to stoop to our Lord's ordained symbols, or by the breaking of bread to show forth his death.

Source: William Arthur, *The Tongue of Fire*, London 1856, pp. 65, 90.

Arthur does not see the permanent benefits of Pentecost to the church as portents or wonders, but as spiritual gifts and graces, communion with God, the victory of truth, the progress of the Divine life and grace among men and women, the joy and assurance of believers, the soul-converting power of ministers [30]. He looks forward with the optimism of grace and of a Victorian Englishman to the conversion of the whole world. But the secret is 'Remember the ten days' – 'They continued with one accord in prayer and supplication.'

The very moderation of *The Tongue of Fire* points to the difficulties of the Methodist position,

---

30. When a lecturer on electricity wants to show an example of a human body surcharged with his fire, he places a person on a stool with glass legs. The glass serves to isolate him from the earth, because it will not conduct the fire – the electric fluid: were it not for this, however much might be poured into his frame, it would be carried away by the earth but, when thus isolated from it, he retains all that enters him. You see no fire, you hear no fire; but you are told that it is pouring into him. Presently you are challenged to the proof – asked to come near, and hold your hand close to his person: when you do so, the spark of fire shoots out towards you. If thou then, wouldst have thy soul surcharged with the fire of God so that those who come nigh thee shall feel some mysterious influence proceeding out from thee, thou must draw nigh to the source of that fire, to the throne of God and of the Lamb, and shut thyself out from the world – that cold world which so swiftly steals our fire away. Enter into thy closet, and shut to thy door, and there, isolated 'before the throne', await the baptism; then the fire shall fill thee, and when thou comest forth, holy power will attend thee, and thou shalt labour not in thine own strength, but with demonstration of the Spirit and with power.

As this is the only way for an individual to obtain spiritual power, so it is the only way for Churches. Prayer, prayer, all prayer – mighty, importunate, repeated, united prayer; the rich and the poor, the learned and the unlearned, the fathers and the children, the Pastors and the people, the gifted and the simple, all uniting to cry to God above, that He would come and affect them as in the days of the right hand of the Most High, and imbue them with the Spirit of Christ, and warm them, and kindle them, and make them as a flame of fire, and lay His right hand mightily on the sinners that surround them, and turn them in truth to Him. Such united and repeated supplications will assuredly accomplish their end, and 'the power of God' descending will make every such company as a band of giants refreshed with new wine.

Source: William Arthur, *The Tongue of Fire*, London 1856, pp. 195–96.

Pentecostalist with a difference, convinced that the world must and will be won for Christ, theoretically organized to assist that sublime purpose, yet shy of extremes, aware of corybantic dangers and of the peculiar risk of charity being the first victim of evangelical fervour. In the second half of the century there were wings of Methodism associated with movements very much peripheral to the great organized confessions, yet numerous and active.

Beginning of the Holiness Movement

The preaching of holiness was even more vigorous in America than in Great Britain. In his essay in *The History of American Methodism*, Timothy L. Smith describes the crusade in the twenty-five years before the outbreak of the Civil War. This owed much to a remarkable Methodist woman, Phoebe Palmer, a doctor's wife from New York City, authoress of innumerable tracts. It was, as Smith says, a concomitant of revivalism, of fervent preaching and mass conversions. Sinners were converted on an instant by the onrush of inexplicable, soul-tearing power; could not saints be similarly perfected? But Smith mentions other factors. 'The ethical ideals to which Emerson and Henry David Thoreau aspired on a highly sophisticated level, plain men of the times sought at a Methodist mourners bench or class-meeting. Entire sanctification was a kind of evangelical transcendentalism which thrived amid the optimism, the idealism and the moral earnestness which were so much a part of nineteenth-century American character'.[14]

The holiness movement was by no means indifferent to the social implications of the doctrine of perfect love. But it had its dangers. The idea of a 'second blessing', of perfection received in a moment, though Wesley must be held to some extent responsible for it, seriously upset the balance of his true teaching which in its dependence on the spirituality of the great masters of the Eastern and Western Church, understands holiness much more in terms of the growth of an organism. In the metaphor of Macarius the Egyptian, previously quoted, perfection is not

'Off with one coat and on with another'. Moreover, there was the likelihood that emotional excitement would be mistaken for ethical change and Mount Carmel obscured: cf. I Corinthians 13.

Patterns of Christian experience

From the biographies of nineteenth-century Methodists there emerges a pattern of Christian experience, which is not peculiar to Methodism, but was the common evangelical scheme. Granted that the home was Christian, the young child would be brought early to conviction of sin often under the ministry of a revivalist preacher such as the Irish Gideon Ouseley, whose *Life* William Arthur wrote. There would be many tears, those infant cries and sobs which John Bunyan had felt were among the most blessed of all sounds. But, later on, in youth, there would be as likely as not a period of degeneration, a falling from grace, perhaps through a vicious school, or wild companions, from which another revivalist was needed to bring recovery. After this there was often no looking back. The Christian was committed to a life of service which would absorb every waking moment if he were a travelling preacher and all his leisure if he were not. Wesley's own full life was repeated in scores of his successors. And this intense dedication was nourished by a life of prayer. Wesley's own rule of early rising was encouraged by numerous exemplars, as indeed it was demanded by the conditions of rural and industrial labour. There would be Sunday morning prayer meetings in the chapels at six or seven o'clock, and beforehand, the devout would be on their knees in private. 'Closet work', as it was somewhat quaintly called, was the duty and the joy of the true Methodist. After he had finished his working life, 'Praying William' would be upstairs at 11, 2, and 6 each day in obedience to Matthew 6.6 and doubtless also Daniel 6.19. Often he would stump down exclaiming, 'O it has been precious! precious! precious! Bless Him! Bless Him!'[15]

This prayer was described also as heart-work in language which could echo Richard Baxter's tribute to George Herbert ('Heart-work and heaven-work make up his books'). The periphrasis is eloquent of the passion and love of Christ and humanity which inspired the prayer and marked it off from all the tedious formalism of fussy and overloaded schemes of devotion.

Fasting was practised both privately and by connexional injunction, and there is no doubt that all those who were serious about their religion obeyed without demur.

Theology of the heart

But the cry was always 'Revival'. On 28 January, 1843, there was printed in Leeds *A Pastoral Letter on the Revival of Religion Addressed Especially to the Wesleyan Methodists*. It is this tract which speaks of 'heart-work', and appeals for a theology of the heart in which truth will be seen not as the test of orthodoxy and the weapon of controversy but as the means of salvation and the rule of holy living. Revivals, it is argued, are always necessary, because 'No human provision can be made against the secret encroachment of a spirit of merely speculative inquiry'.

The main burden is a series of very practical counsels to revive the church, though it is asserted that 'our beloved Connexion' is in no sense approaching a period of decay.' We have nothing to fear from outward opposition from any quarter, so long as we maintain the purity of our doctrine, the vigour of our moral and religious discipline, the possession and practice of real holiness and the energy and simplicity of our zeal in seeking the conversion of the world.'

These may be maintained as individual members show a deep concern about religion, 'parents begin to pray for and with their children', brothers and sisters, masters and servants. The question should always be, not 'How did you like the sermon?' but 'Did you profit by it?' All the work of the church should be supported and cottage prayer meetings attended, tracts distributed, and help should be given with the religious instruction of the children of the poor. A resolve should be made to bring one additional person each quarter to class, one additional hearer to worship. The pledges of the Covenant Service are quoted.

Finally there is a Wesleyan insistence on the linking of prayer and faith with the *means* of grace, both instituted and prudential as Wesley, following Nelson, had distinguished them. Reading is included in the latter, particularly the lives of eminent ministers, such as the American Calvinist Jonathan Edwards, and histories. One detects that in the Wesleyan body there was a certain disdain of what Augustine called 'the sacraments of the humility of God's word'.

Class meetings and the good old fashioned church meetings and Love Feasts must not be neglected out of snobbishness. 'A fastidious taste may take offence at what is there spoken; but if so, the fact shows that the heart needs mending.' In all this Wesley, being dead yet speaks.

For discussion

1. Are revivals always necessary in the life of the church?
2. Are regular habits essential for the life of prayer? How may they be acquired?
3. Could you spend a whole day or night in prayer? Have you experience of the fervour of Mow Cop? Or of being unable to tear yourself away from prayer?
4. Is there too much emphasis on 'the Quiet Time' in prayer? Must there not sometimes be both an excited rapturous awareness of God's presence and 'a storming of the heavens'?
5. It is now apparent that William Arthur was vehemently anti-Catholic. Ireland may have had something to do with it, but is not *The Tongue of Fire* more compatible with Catholicism than the constant cry of 'Revival'?

11

The Family

In no sense were the Methodists more the heirs of Puritanism than in their constant stress on the importance of family life and the household as the nursery of the church. *A Plan of Scripture Reading for Family Worship* was published by Charles Atmore at Halifax in 1813. He writes with the confidence of approaching victory in the Napoleonic Wars. England will be saved by a praying remnant. He quotes the Puritan, Oliver Heywood: 'When public persecutions break up Church assemblies family worship will maintain religion in the world. When ministers were banished (and he spoke feelingly being one of the banished ones himself) assemblies scattered, and churches demolished still the fire glowed hot on private hearths.'

Christian marriage

There was much good advice on the choice of marriage partners. 'If possible,' writes Dr Walsh in his essay on 'Methodism at the end of the Eighteenth Century', 'Methodist married Methodist, remembering St Paul's injunction to the Corinthians, "be not unequally yoked with unbelievers".'[1] A hundred years later this was still the hope. One of my grandfather William Henry Spooner's manuscript addresses to his Society class was given, so he notes, under the title, 'The Twelfth Commandment'; this is, according to him, another saying of St Paul that marriage be 'only in the Lord' (I Cor. 7.30).

31. When e'er by noxious cares oppressed
On the soft pillow of her breast
    My aching head I'd lay.
At her sweet smile each care shall cease
Her kiss infuse a balmy peace
    And drive my tears away.

Together would we meekly bend
Together should our prayers ascend
    To praise the Almighty's name.
And when I saw her kindling eye
Beat upward to her native sky
    My soul should catch the flame.

Thus nothing should our hearts divide
But on our years serenely glide
    And all to love be given.
And when life's little scene was o'er
We'd part to meet and part no more
    But live and love in heaven.

Source: Mss of William Henry Spooner. Author unknown.

My grandfather's exegesis leaves much to be desired, since Paul is in fact writing of the remarriage of Christian widows (which he is inclined not to advise), and the chapter is concerned entirely with the situation of Christians in Corinth in the middle years of the first century and the problem of the mixed marriages of Christians and pagans. It is saturated with an eschatology very different from the

Victorian. But Spooner makes his point with scriptural and contemporary illustrations. To take an ungodly wife (or husband) is 'this sin of sins, this crime of crimes'. There is a vehement attack on the deceitfulness of men, who are far worse than women, including the very questionable statement indicative of the Victorian attitude to women when make-up was reserved for theatricals, women of high society or of dubious morals: 'We don't often find young ladies attiring just to please their suitors, but men often put on a false exterior to deceive innocent girls.' There is a lurid concluding story of a Methodist minister's daughter, who, against all advice, married an ungodly man. Before long she was made ill by her husband's cruelty and the narrative passes into the present tense to recount the pitiful end: 'A broken-hearted father endeavours to point a wayward child to a deserted heavenly father and oh! the last words she utters they rend that father's heart and how they make one shudder at their awful import – "I can't get over the gulf" she exclaims and dies'. But, earlier, the class leader quotes stanzas in imitation of Charles Wesley [31].

Praying together

Family prayers were assumed as the framework of the Christian home. Methodism did not confine public religious services to the Lord's day; there was not quite the Puritan assumption that on the six days of labour the church was the house; Methodists used their chapels for mid-week meetings for prayer, class, preaching and revival. But it was expected that public worship and private prayer should be assisted by what was done in the family, which in its ideal was not so very different from what Burns describes in 'The Cotter's Saturday Night' [32]. 'Praying William' once refused a holiday which some friends were willing to provide for him: 'No! No! I cannot go; for if I go, who will pray night and morning with my poor children.'

It was hoped and prayed that through the family influence children might early be won for Christ. I remember an octogenarian lady in my first circuit in the mid-1940s, who told me how her mother, a Yorkshire Primitive Methodist, a charwoman and very poor, would go each week to the chapel prayer-meeting and ask that her children 'might see the king in his beauty'. The pre-natal period was reckoned , after Aristotle, to be of supreme importance in shap-

---

32. Then kneeling down to Heaven's Eternal King
The saint, the father and the husband prays:
Hope 'springs exulting on triumphant wing'
That thus they all shall meet in future days
No more to sigh or shed the bitter tear,
Together hymning their Creator's praise,
In such society, yet still more dear:
While circling Time moves round in an eternal
sphere.

Source: Robert Burns, 'The Cotter's Saturday Night' (*c.*1785).

---

ing a child's character, inclinations and destiny. Thomas Collins' biographer writes of the 'precious pre-consecration of life by maternal purpose and prayer'.[2]

My own mother never ceased to believe that I became a minister because during her pregnancy she had been a class leader engaged in regular study and preparation which included the reading of Milton (perhaps with the half-conscious hope that I should be, not a minister, but a man of letters).

Childhood piety

There was in nineteenth-century Methodism a tradition of the Christian child, dedicated, precocious and like as not sickly. The type owes its existence not simply to family religion but to the illness and mortality rate in the new industrial society whose *laissez-faire* system could not cope with its problems and where disease was not properly understood.

In Manchester there was first published in 1827 a little book destined to go through five editions.

EXAMPLES OF EARLY PIETY
Written for the Benefit of Children
and
Encouragement of Parents
Consisting of Memoirs
of
JAMES B. JONES
and a Brief Notice of
ELIZABETH E. JONES
by their Father

Mr Jones Snr was a Wesleyan minister; neither of his children reached adolescence. The boy, James, was a solemn though loving child, who once moved his father by embracing him with the words 'I love you, Papa, and I love God Almighty: and when I go to the heaven I'll kiss Him too.'

Needless to say, the boy was delicate and one winter he and his sister were both very ill. The girl died, but James survived to endure an appalling erysipelas. His talk was mostly of heaven, though he admitted once that eternity was a subject that he could not comprehend and he was much puzzled by the thought of going on for ever. Yet on his birthday, as he lay watching his birthday cake being cut up for his friends (I opine mostly adults), he said, 'The day of my death will be better than the day of my birth. God loves me and has pardoned my sins.' He took time in her presence to express some doubts as to the spiritual state of a young woman who had come to visit him ('Miss S. is not quite *right*') then he went on: 'Mine is an affecting case, but at the same time it is a glorious one. Who would have thought that God would be so kind to such a little boy as I am. I am so happy! O I am very happy. I wish you would tell other little boys how good the Lord has been to me; perhaps it may do them good; perhaps they may also come to the Lord Jesus Christ and be happy also.'

He suggested that they sing a hymn; and they did, from Charles Wesley:

> O disclose thy lovely face!
> Quicken all my drooping powers.
> Gasps my fainting soul for grace

> As a thirsty land for showers;
> Haste, my Lord, no more delay.
> Come, my Saviour, come away.

with its echo of Augustine's *Confessions* in the second verse:

> Well Thou knowest I cannot rest
> Till I fully rest in Thee . . .[3]

A week or two later James B. Jones died. He was just nine.[4]

Sometimes the child would grow up but be stricken by consumption or cholera very early in manhood. Most societies had their memories of such and often they were renowned for the love of Jesus and for promise unfulfilled. In his manuscript book, William Henry Spooner has copied some verses by his brother George, who died in his early twenties. They are conventional enough and imperfect, but interesting, since they come from the grass roots and state very simply the evangelical faith and hope of a young man with but a short time to live. They show, too, that the hymnbook tradition was still alive and it was natural for Methodists, even the humbler ones without any particular genius, to express themselves in verse [33]. Some familiar Methodist notes are there: 'I'll praise my Maker while I've breath' for instance, and the evangelical conviction of sin and of wandering, but to be holy is to be fit for heaven rather than to be made perfect in love. Heaven indeed was even more a preoccupation than in a century earlier and, if it comes to that, nineteenth-century preachers probably had more to say about hell than did Wesley.

Sabbath observance

The great cornerstone of family as it was of national religion was the observance of Sunday, called by the devout, the sabbath. This again was Puritan, and the doctrine propagated by Nicholas Bownde in 1595 that the Christian Sunday is virtually the same as the

33.   *Returning to Jesus*

Jesus again I'll fly to Thee
And give my wanderings o'er;
For Thou hast died on Calvary,
And Thou my sin hast bore.

Now Lord receive Thy wand'ring child
Who far from Thee hath gone;
Come Jesus pityful and mild,
And claim me as Thine own.

Repentance, faith and pardon give
And also give me grace;
And make me fit in heaven to live
Where I may see Thy face.

Now that I can my pardon claim,
Through Jesus' painful death,
I'll always try to speak His fame,
As long as I have breath.

Source: Mss of William Henry Spooner. Verses by George Spooner.

Jewish sabbath went on its triumphant course in British Christianity.[5]

Stories were told of judgments on sabbath breakers very reminiscent of Lewis Bayly's admonitory example in *The Practice of Piety* (1612) which, after all, was issued for the last time as late as 1842. A dissolute young man, for instance, might be brought to a sense of sin through a storm buffeting the boat in

34.   The gay who rest nor worship prize
Jehovah's changeless sign despise.
Still stand it to our eyes alone
With claims and blessings all its own.

The suffering scarce, alas! can know
This from the other days of woe.
May we the worth of Sabbaths learn
Before we suffer in our turn.

Source: *Methodist Hymn Book*, 1904, No. 638.

which he had sailed to illicit sabbath pleasures. So wrote William Maclardie Bunting, son of Jabez, in a hymn which survived until 1933 [34]. (He did write better hymns than this, such as 'Blessed are the pure in heart', though even here there is a sabbatarian verse.) In the library of the Leys School at Cambridge there are still works classified as 'suitable for reading on Sunday' by the imprimatur of the clerical headmaster who retired in 1934.

The Methodist Victorian sabbath does not need defence. The technological revolution bids fair to obliterate what the industrial revolution largely spared. But for the Methodist working men of last century Sunday was at once the beginning and the crown of the work. 'Now we have done with the world till Monday morning,' the missioner Lax of Poplar's father would cry as he finished work on Saturday. Shoes were cleaned and food prepared so that all unnecessary duties could be avoided on the Lord's day. Sunday trains were considered to be the start of the journey to hell, a most wicked apostasy. John Newton's Olney hymn for Saturday evening, commended earlier by Mrs William Wilberforce to her son, Samuel, at university, was in the Methodist hymn book still in 1904, and was sung by the students of Southlands college in the 1880s [35].

35.   Safely through another week
God hath brought us on our way.
Let us now a blessing seek
On the approaching Sabbath day.
Day of all the week the best
Emblem of eternal rest.

Source: *Methodist Hymn Book*, 1904, No. 929.

Rest or no, the sabbath was a long day for the Society leader or local preacher, or for the 'enquirer' (the equivalent perhaps of the catechumen) . 'Praying William' had been drunken and profligate in his youth and he was first turned to serious thoughts by going to visit a sick friend and having a conversation about heaven. This and the solemnities of the subsequent funeral drove him to spend Sunday with the Methodists at Norfolk Street Chapel, Sheffield. This meant that on that first occasion he heard three sermons and attended the prayer-meetings, beginning at 6 a.m. But since he believed that his eternal destiny was at stake he could hardly grudge the time or complain that the sermons were too long. Later on, the Methodists whose Sundays were crowded with services and sabbath school and organization would sing lines by one of their famed preachers, William Morley Punshon (1825–81):

> At work for God in loved employ
> We lose the duty in the joy.

This was true to experience in the more prosperous, neo-Gothic churches at the end of the century: among the Methodists of the proletariat, depressed in the middle years, Sunday was a day when the working man was given a place and a voice and made aware of his dignity as a child of God .

For discussion

1. Remembering that Jesus disrupted family life on several occasions, can we still call the family the 'nursery of the church'?

2. Have family prayers declined? If so, why?

3. Has the cult of the 'holy child', often an invalid, disappeared due in part to greater child health? Are children any longer dedicated to God from birth, like Samuel or Jesus?

4. Is Christianity strengthened or weakened by the fact that, for most people, attendance at church and church-based service are no longer their main interests outside their work?

12

A Piety Based on Preaching

The cult of the pulpit

The last fifty years of the nineteenth century was the era of great preachers, and Methodist spirituality was undoubtedly influenced by the cult of the pulpit. This was to some extent a departure from the distinctive Methodist norm, which had conceived of the preacher chiefly as evangelist, often in the open air, and had relied on class meetings more than sermons for the schooling of saints. Thomas Collins' biographer treats himself to one of his lengthy improving asides on this theme [36].

> 36. 'Methodist Preachers!' – the designation suggests our lack while it expresses our power. People say that 'we preach well'. If practice can ensure that, we certainly ought to do so. The inexorable demands of Methodism are more numerous than those of any Church in Christendom; but is preaching everything? ... But venerable and honourable as is their appellation (Methodist Preachers) it is neither older nor better than 'Pastors and teachers' of Eph. IV,11 ... The lambs will never be fed by a mere sermon mill. Hooker says 'The delivery of the elements should be framed to the slender capacity of beginners.' They must be catechized.
>
> *Source:* Samuel Coley, *The Life of the Revd Thomas Collins,* London 1896, pp. 95–96.

In *The Tongue of Fire,* William Arthur contrasts the convention of his own time with the religion of Pentecost, which made all Christians witnesses [37].

> 37. Looking on the universal movement of that Pentecostal day who will think that the new religion was ever to come down to this, that speaking of its joys, its hopes, its pardon, its mercy for the wide world was to be considered a professional work for set solemnities alone, and not be a daily joy and heart's ease to ever growing multitudes of happy simple men?
>
> *Source*: William Arthur, *The Tongue of Fire,* London 1856, pp. 95–96.

'Let them ask if it is like their religion that one lonely minister shall, on the Lord's day, bear witness before a thousand Christians, who decorously hear his testimony as worthy of acceptance by all, and then go away and never repeat the strain in any human ear?'

Be that as it may, by the end of the century Methodism was little distinguishable from the other Free Churches, as they were now to be called, in the belief that the strength of Christianity was to be measured by the large congregation hanging on the words of a preacher, whose sermons were 'less patient and formal expositions' than 'red-hot exhortation and dramatic religious demagogy'.[1] There was some attempt, as Routley has said, 'to reproduce under cover of a roof the open-air evangelism of the Wesleys' and the massed congregations of the Methodists, especially in the new Central Halls, were likely to include a much larger proportion of artisans and poorer people than those of the other Free Churches.

The sermon as a means of instruction

The effect on the spiritual life and its patterns was considerable. On the face of it a popular sermon may not seem a very good medium for spiritual direction, and certainly the modern fashion has been to despise it in the name of sound educational method, though this in turn is now suspected as a synonym for the latest fad of our pedagogic conditioners. But the sermon has a long history as a primary means of instruction,[2] and those who went to Central Halls on Sunday nights or suburban churches on Sunday mornings may well have received understanding of the gospel and help in Christian living through the sermon which 'group dynamics' would not have given them.

For one thing it may not be physically possible to organize a thousand people in classes; for another, there are many who do not respond to group methods, who may learn something from a sermon. The danger is that 'rostrum Christianity' may be wanton, heretical and narrow. Great problems may be brushed aside by a few cheap illustrations or rhetorical phrases, public taste rather than truth may dictate what is said, and the preacher governed by the desire to find favour and maintain crowds may be led into an utter loss of integrity. The desire to give people a secure and strong faith and never to undermine their confidence that 'God's in his heaven all's right with the world' is in many ways admirable, but breeds distrust in the next generation.

Alternatively, the abstract denunciation of social evils without a genuine and sympathetic understanding of their cause or knowledge of their cure is an inveterate danger, whether those evils be drink, prostitution, segregation, or war. More and more the distance between the sermon and the life of the world increases, and going to church becomes an activity of the twilight, or a dream which dies at the opening day. A pulpit style and a language are handed down which, though less ugly than the jargon of our scientific culture and no harder to understand in themselves, sound hollow, meaningless, irrelevant and ineffective, appropriate prey for *Beyond the Fringe*, recordings of which began many sermon classes in the 1960s and 1970s. A church whose chief intellectual activity is preaching may substitute declamation for argument, and perorations for scholarship.

Yet since our task is to interpret, not simply to criticize, we must recognize that the increasing belief that the principal religious act of the week was the hearing of a preacher gave to Methodist spirituality a pattern of its own with which other Free Churches may not have been so deeply stamped, since preaching for them was not to the same extent shared by laymen, or women. The instance of Dinah Morris in George Eliot's *Adam Bede* is even more significant than that of the more settled pastor-preachers.

The sermon as meditation

But a sermon is a form of meditation and the assembled congregation was really being taught this technique without knowing it. Perhaps the connection was not always made plain, but in fact if the hearer had applied the method of the Sunday sermon to his own private reading of the scriptures he would have been engaged in a classic Catholic activity of the spiritual life. If he had completed his exercise with a Wesley hymn he might have been brought to the verge of contemplation. What is more, 'A Methodist layman may spend much of his leisure time preparing a sermon or Sunday school lesson or thinking what he is to say to his class; he may never think about the methods of meditation; but he sits with his Bible or his hymn-book in his hand actually meditating.'[3]

The piety of the sermon meant that the Methodist images were mental and verbal, not visual. The chapels of the later Victorian era were more 'decorated' than those of the earlier period, but there was a reluctance to co-ordinate church design with worship. It was by no means assumed that an Anglican-type building would mean a Prayer Book service;

indeed the buildings, as with the other Free Churches, were first and foremost status symbols. Crosses and simple ceremonial crept in very gradually to public worship, to a large extent after 1945, and for some decades there were Methodists who would encourage in the Sunday school what they abominated in church. This was not detestable inconsistency, rather a Puritan belief that the full grown person in Christ should have put away childish things. The Methodist eschewed visual aids in worship for the same reason that he closed his eyes in prayer; he would have found them distracting. The wonder of the gospel ought to be enough in itself to require no ornament.

This did mean that good Methodists were used to concentrating their minds on the sermon and thinking the preacher's thoughts with him, not always in a mood of submissive acquiescence. Listening to sermons whetted the critical faculties, though often a judgment of content was in fact a judgment of the preacher's personality. The pre-eminence of the sermon could make the rest of the service but 'preliminaries' and it led to a failure to understand liturgy as well as a tyranny of words. It was a rarefied, fastidious and perhaps 'unco guid' Methodist who really appreciated silence. And in the nineteenth century at any rate it was what was heard that moved men and women and brought them into the presence of God.

For discussion

1. Do you gain much from sermons? What do you expect?

2. Has the sermon monologue had too great a place in Methodism as William Arthur and others thought? What techniques are necessary as well?

3. Are you able to name preachers who have had a decisive influence on your life and thought?

13

Cheerfulness Breaking In

The Methodist life in the nineteenth century was narrow by twentieth-century standards, as it was bound to be until the church could be fertilized by the universities. The Education Act of 1871 has over the years transformed English dissent; perhaps it killed it. John Kent has written of the historical autonomy of Methodism in the 1850s: 'It contained thousands of people for whom life was a Wesleyan creation, who saw the surrounding world through Wesleyan spectacles, for whom the future of Wesleyan Methodism mattered far more than the fate of secular empires far away in a different dimension'.[1] Any other Methodist name could be substituted for Wesleyan. By the end of the century, Methodists were becoming more concerned in the wider political and social issues of the world, but in 1890 Richard Green, though convinced that Methodism would always be needed, had to admit that it 'may not be adapted to meet the preferences of the people of the country generally . . . It may lack the necessary comprehensiveness.'[2]

There is something majestic about late Victorian Methodist piety, which reached into the next century, even in its narrowness. A friend has told me how as a boy he was once staying in the home of his grandfather, a Methodist minister, and a vivacious young aunt brought a pack of playing cards and was teaching him to play. When the grandfather discovered them at their game, he not only delivered a stern and sorrowful reproof, but retired to his study and spent two hours wrestling in prayer for their salvation.

A life outside

At the same time, the life of the Methodist people was not completely circumscribed by work and chapel. Nature interested them and many became students of flowers, trees, birds and butterflies. A walk with my grandfather in the lanes around West Bromwich, such as they were, was a lesson in botany, and there was a revered old gentleman in my home church, as cultured as he was devout, who had a vast collection of butterflies. The study of the Bible itself led them to history, archaeology and languages. My grandfather talked to his class about the manners and customs of ancient Egyptians as well as about saving faith, about scientists and the speed of light as well as unconditional election, while preserved in his manuscript book itself are some threads of glass fibre. W. H. Dallinger, a Wesleyan minister who died in 1909, was a Fellow of the Royal Society, and a household name among the better informed older Wesleyans of my boyhood. From 1888, he was set apart by Conference to develop his work on the 'biology of micro-organisms'. As late as 1940, I heard him cited in a sermon as having demonstrated beyond all doubt that 'all life was derived'. He was in some sense a precursor of the elegant and liberal Charles Coulson, Rouse Ball Professor of Mathematics at Oxford, Vice President of Conference in 1959, who did much to reconcile Christianity and science in the years after 1950.[3]

Methodists became interested in sport and were

to take their share in the new world of mass-entertainment in the twentieth century.

Assurance of God's favour

The characteristic note of Methodism was still cheerfulness. The *Class-Leader's Assistant*, published in 1857, declares that Christians must not hang down their heads or have quivering lips. They must rejoice in their religion, and this they will do because a good conscience gives them the assurance of the favour of God and an interest in heaven. The manual goes on to quote a recent hymn (1847) by Mary Peters (née Bowley). She was in fact an Anglican married to a Gloucestershire incumbent, but it is interesting and appropriate that Methodists should find it congenial, for inartistic jingle as it is, it directly echoes Julian of Norwich [38].

---

38. Through the love of God our Saviour,
     All will be well;
     Free and changeless is His favour,
     All, all is well:
     Precious is the blood that healed us;
     Perfect is the grace that sealed us,
     Strong the hand stretched forth to shield us,
     All must be well.

Source: *Methodist Hymn Book*, 1933, No. 525.

Holiness is happiness

This joy and confidence was based on a desperate conscientiousness; it could be stern. An early lesson for each child was that 'to obey is best' and more than one Victorian Methodist mother would have endorsed Susanna Wesley's words about breaking the child's will. Yet the reward of goodness was presented as a happiness beyond this world altogether, which amid all the vicissitudes of life would never fail since its source was unclouded communion with the Saviour. No more than Wesley did Methodists indulge the belief that the Christian might need to pass through a 'wilderness state' of doubt and dereliction. I myself knew a Northumbrian miner who always refused to sing William Cowper's lines:

> Where is the blessedness I knew
> When first I saw the Lord?

because he believed that if a Christian was faithful, his joy in Christ would never diminish, nor the vision be clouded. This was undoubtedly his own experience and it was authentically Methodist, but too exceptional to formulate as a universal law of the spiritual life, as the *Class Leader's Assistant* itself implies when it gives some good advice to foster the believer's rejoicing. Answers to prayer must be looked for, the means of grace used, our own weakness of character discerned, prayer for one another in the Society constantly maintained, the longing for heaven kindled. This is classical, and shows that, in practice, the Methodist belief that holiness is happiness did not make them naive, or blunt the edge of their spiritual counsel. But the 'terrible twentieth century' with its moral and scientific earthquakes, in spite of its achievements in making life longer and healthier for some in the west and north, was not only going to break down the old safe fences of religion and culture, but also to leave a *malaise* and a desolation with which the simple piety of Christian joy would not easily cope.

For discussion

1. Has the end of sabbatarianism contributed to the decline of Christianity?

2. Do you believe with Julian of Norwich and Mary Peters that 'All will be well'?

3. Should the Christian live between faith and doubt?

4. Would you agree that 'goodness' and 'holiness' make for happiness?

PART III

THE TWENTIETH CENTURY

14

The Holiness Movement and Responses

There was in the Methodism of the late nineteenth and early twentieth centuries a strong continuing revivalist element, a Holiness Movement seeking to restore Wesley's teaching on perfection to its central place. Samuel Chadwick, its outstanding leader, had a vision of 'earnest prayer, living testimony, impassioned enthusiasm, and intense spirituality' through which Methodism would 'spread Scriptural holiness throughout the land, evangelize the world and reform the nation'.[1]

Samuel Chadwick and Cliff College

The centre was Cliff College in the Derbyshire Peak District, opened in 1904, under the Principalship of Thomas Cook (1859–1912), a renowned evangelist and preacher of entire sanctification. He was continuing work begun by Thomas Champness (1832–1904) and his wife Eliza, who in the 1880s began training lay evangelists, known as 'Joyful News Evangelists'. They started, in 1883, a weekly paper called *Joyful News*, modelled on the Salvation Army's *War Cry*, which soon reached a circulation of 30,000.

Cliff College continued Champness's work of giving some book learning and practical guidance to those who would otherwise have had little chance of them but it also, from 1926, under Chadwick, provided a base from which Franciscan type trekkers might go out on special tasks of evangelism.

Samuel Chadwick (1860–1932) soon became the dominant revivalist leader. He had been made aware of the power of holiness teaching when he heard John Denholm Brash, a very humanist exponent, mentioned below, in 1883. His own ministry was transformed and he began to make converts. He had a most successful ministry at Oxford Place, Leeds, known to the northern populace at large, subject of topical reference by comedians on Blackpool sea front. He became editor of *Joyful News*. In 1907 he was made biblical and theological tutor at Cliff College and succeeded as Principal on Cook's early death in 1912. Cliff College became a kind of extension of Chadwick's personality.

There were revivalist scenes – an algebra class was suspended at the college in 1920 with exclamations of 'Alleluia' and 'Glory has come into my soul' – and many successful missions. Chadwick believed in the early 1920s that revival would sweep the country. But it did not. There is a poignancy about the passionate longings, the partial successes and the ultimate failure, the country drifting ever more into secularism, the churches in slow decline.

The Southport Convention was another instrument of revival and holiness of which Chadwick was the moving spirit. To some extent it was in rivalry with the Keswick Convention which came from a more Calvinist evangelicalism and to which Chadwick was never invited. Southport stood for 'the doctrine of the *eradication* of inbred sin and *imparted* holiness, as against the Keswick teaching of *repression* of sin and *imputed* holiness'.

Chadwick and his adjutants believed that there was a second crisis by which a person might enter into entire sanctification. His successor at Cliff, J. A. Broadbelt, described in the *Joyful News* of 20

October 1932 a 'revelation' he had received that the Spirit could make a person 'free from the law of sin and death' . This was not only a second blessing but a bigger experience than the first experience of grace. This, it was said, was Methodism's 'audacious claim'. 'Perfect love and scriptural holiness proclaim a perfect Salvation'. Belief in a second work of grace which instantly purified the heart was reiterated in the 1930s by J. I. Brice, editor of Chadwick's last book on Perfection, who ended his ministry as an extreme Anglo-Catholic priest in Northumberland and Norfolk, where he is still remembered. Ian Randall has shown how there were parallel movements in the Salvation Army and on the evangelical fringes. The Pentecostal League of Prayer was founded by a Queen's Counsel, Richard Reeder Harris, in 1891. He and his wife claimed entire sanctification. Many controversies and separations ensued, but Chadwick was glad to speak to the League on three occasions – 'Everything Pentecostalist appeals to me' – and Broadbelt was for a time a member. Other bodies laid stress on healing, holiness involving wholeness, the entire person and revival meeting the criteria of the longer ending of Mark's Gospel.

Looking to the past

Perhaps the failure – or at least the very partial success – of this movement was due to the fact that it was backward-looking, forever seeking to return to a past age of revival, of which the power, though great, was nonetheless exaggerated. It was not adequate in its understanding of the new, post-war age, as though those strange voices could be drowned by revivalist alleluias. Nor did it have a sufficient understanding of the church, the nature of which was becoming prominent on the Christian agenda as the ecumenical movement gained strength. It was increasingly impossible not to be aware of other communions and the need of catholicity, a faith true to Christian origins and alive to the needs of the world The veteran Methodist leader, John Scott Lidgett, first President of the United Conference of 1932, had catholicity as his watchword and devoted his presidential address to the Nicene Creed. Broadbelt was convinced of the need to found holiness teaching on sound scholarship, and encouraged Maurice Barnett, destined to become minister of Westminster Central Hall, and others to obtain a full gamut of Manchester Divinity degrees. There was in those days confidence that genuine academic study could not but confirm faith. It was not conceived that, undertaken with devotion and integrity it could expose Christianity's vulnerability. All the same, revivalism persisted and knew success in the Billy Graham campaigns as it does in the Spring Harvest and the Easter People movements and the Toronto Blessing. But these are manifestations of an evangelicalism which does not take its stand on confessional beliefs. It is not distinctively Methodist. Expectations of nation-wide revival may be lower, years of evangelism – and decades – are at a discount, as are week's missions, but the evangelical strain is loudest in contemporary Christianity. This is different from the middle decades of the century, in spite of Graham. There is a social conscience as well as an individual emphasis. Evangelicalism always tends to be fissiparous. There is a 'holier than thou' element and the charismatic movement divides. Holiness is perhaps less prominent except at Cliff College. It is more a Catholic than an evangelical emphasis. The problem is relating Christianity to modern culture to which it appears alien.

For discussion

1. Has the fact that Methodism began as a revival of religion diverted its subsequent history, so that false hopes have been raised and there has been expectation that a church true to its vocation would see a repetition of the eighteenth century which, in a different age, is not possible?

2. What characteristics and convictions in a Christian are necessary to make converts?

3. Is it possible to think of the Jesus of the Gospels as our friend now?

15

The Liberal Reaction

There were many Methodists who were unhappy with revivalism and the Holiness Movement, especially with the 'aggressive evangelicalism' which dragooned people to the penitent form. The young Newton Flew, who later was to speak at the Southport Convention, and enjoy his visit to Cliff College as President of Conference in 1947, wrote a letter from his first church, deploring the action of one of his colleagues at a ministerial convention [39].

> 39. The man had spoken not without sense on entire sanctification. But he ends up by asking all who want to claim the blessing straight away to come out and line up in front, takes the meeting out of the Super's hands, lines up himself, dragoons two or three more hoary old saints out of their seats ... two or three trembling girls and has a high old time procuring the second blessing for these lined up sinners. God forgive me but I do not like this way and fall into profanity when I think about it. Were Peter and John and the rest lined up in front on the day of Pentecost? Was our founder lined up in Aldersgate Street? ... Must I verily line up if I want to see the Lord? Ah, no, verily but it is hard for those who love him in sincerity and passion to see misguided fanatics come along, torture sensitive hearts, spoil meetings aflame with desire, and try to force every experience on to the Procrustean bed of their own narrow holiness.
>
> When will these fellows learn something of the awe, the tenderness, the delicacy, the mysterious issues which belong to the ministry of souls?
>
> *Source*: Letter from Newton Flew to his mother, 4 October 1915.

Perfect love

Flew strongly believed that the Methodist teaching of perfect love should be revived and restated. He won his Oxford DD – the first non-Anglican to do so by examination – for a study of *The Idea of Perfection in Christian Theology* (1934). He examines and criticizes the treatment of Perfection in the writings of twenty-one different periods of church history with especial attention to developments within Protestantism. The Eastern Orthodox teaching and much of the Catholic Reformation are lacking, and more recent scholarship would revise some of the opinions. He concludes that 'the seeing of an ideal that is realizable in this world is essential to Christianity' and establishes eight principles of a positive doctrine, which we summarize as follows:

1. The Christian ideal must span both worlds and must recognize their inter-relationship.
2. The Christian life is the gift of God.
3. No limits can be set to the moral or spiritual attainment of a Christian in this life. There must always be a 'beyond'. 'The one person who cannot be perfect is the person who claims to be.'
4. The good life has many realms: it is a social life and includes the pursuit of truth and beauty as well as moral goodness.
5. Daily work is a divine vocation.
6. The ideal life is 'Moment-by-moment holiness'. Here Flew introduces a theme prominent in de Caussade (1675–1751), *L'Abandon á la Providence Divin*. The English Benedictine Dom John

Chapman made this discovery towards the end of his tortured course.

7. There must be a sense of personal unworthiness.
8. There is no escaping the Cross: 'the dying out of the temporal realm into the eternal'.[1]

---

40. Our theological coat (says a modern Methodist) was cut for the figure of Total Depravity, but when it was tried on, it was found not to fit any kind of human nature. Accordingly we let out a seam in the back, as far as it would go, and the margin thus gained with the stitches still showing, we called prevenient grace. Still the coat does not fit, for it is not by any afterthought that we can do justice to that boundless patience and holiness of God, which loves goodness everywhere, labours for it and delights in it everywhere. We have often thought of God as though it were 'all or nothing' with him. But it is not true. In His mysterious humility He tends the last smouldering lamp in every rebellious heart ... It is he who defends the last strip of territory against the invasion of passion, when all the rest is gone, and raises mysterious defences about beleaguered virtues whose doom seemed sure. When He is denied or unrecognized in His own person, He still lingers about a man, dimly apprehended as a sense of duty, or as some indestructible principle, some notion of what is 'not cricket', some code of thieves, or He returns upon us in some New Thought, some shadow Infinite, some impersonal Life-Force, some half-crazy system like Christian Science, worshipping its fragment of the truth - and so men entertain Him unawares. These vast tracts of the unbaptized human lives we make over to poets, and novelists and dramatists who explore them with inexhaustible interest and sympathy. Yet this interest and sympathy come from God, who loves this human-life of ours, not only as a moralist, approving where it is good and disproving where it is bad, but as a poet or artist loves it, because he cannot help loving a thing so strange, piteous and enthralling as the story of every human soul must be.

Source: W. R. Maltby in the *Methodist Recorder* December 1916. See Flew, *The Idea of Perfection in Christian Theology*, OUP 1934, pp. 340–41.

Flew has many criticisms of Wesley's teaching; some are those noted above. He maintains that 'The vision of God granted to men in Wesley's day was not equal to the revelation of Him in the first three Gospels, if it be true that God is what Jesus is in his inexhaustible interest in human life.' He ends the book with a quotation from an article by William Russell Maltby [40].

Some might think that eighty years on this fine passage does not fully reckon with the hideous reality of evil in our human life.

The reality of human life

Maltby was the master of a group of ministers, which included J. Alexander Findlay, and Leslie Weatherhead as well as Flew. Their concept of holiness was different from that of Samuel Chadwick, who had no interest in games and lamented that churches had become social clubs with billiards and snooker predominating and operettas replacing prayer meetings. Flew and company held as an example of Christian perfection the very John Denholm Brash (1841–1912) who had so influenced Chadwick in the 1880s. He was debating the selection of the English test team in his last illness a few days before his death. 'He would speak about Christ and cricket in the same breath, and about cricket averages and the missionary problems. He was also interested in football, athletics and golf.'[2]

In *The Significance of Jesus*, first published in 1948, Maltby criticizes Jeremy Taylor's *Holy Living* because it laments the time we must spend 'in eating and drinking ... in necessary business and unnecessary vanities, in worldly civilities and less useful circumstance, in the learning arts, languages, sciences or trades'. Taylor does not help us to see that 'the appointments of this earthly life ... are of God and therefore have love and have friendly significance in themselves' [41].

Even in those days, some might have thought that Maltby was insufficiently aware of 'dead-end' jobs of soul-destroying, boring, mechanical tasks in which it

41. So someone has said: If I am in the cotton business and feel the zest of it, does God feel any interest like my own? If I struggle with my picture and at last get my bit of cloud just right, does God care about that too? Enjoy *Punch* and *Pickwick*. Does God allow me to read them only as a sort of concession to my foolishness? If I mind a machine all day does God care about my bit of skill, my accuracy and deftness? If I make buttons, does God care about buttons? If little boys play football, does God only say, 'little things please little minds?'

Source: W. R. Maltby, *The Significance of Jesus* [1948], reissued Epworth Press 1965, pp. 84–86.

was not easy to be aware of God, though monks and mystics might have made them the accompaniment of meditation. Now manufacturing has changed radically. And football has become an industry with astronomical sums involved and temptations unrealized sixty years ago, while novelists and poets, though often with an understanding of human nature profounder than that of the theologians have, censorship abandoned, become explicitly sexual, some would say pornographic, though some would think the rending of veils healthier than modest concealment. Technology has triumphed over individual skills and the computer dominates increasingly while the cloning of life become possible.

Secular Christianity

Alec Findlay wrote similarly. In his 1950 Fernley-Hartley lecture, he anticipated some of the truer insights of the secular theologians of the 1960s. He foresaw the possible end of 'organized Christianity' and disliked both high churchmanship and clericalism. He sought to free Methodism from the narrowness, the cultural philistinism and the sheer inhumanity of much of what he had known when he was young. His wife and he attracted criticism in one of their last circuits before Didsbury because they sent their daughter to dancing classes. In his Fernley-Hartley lecture he stated:

Something new should be struggling to birth in our perhaps reluctant minds - reluctant because we all like our spiritual food served up on dishes we are accustomed to. Jesus is telling us what God really feels about the jolly, easy going people who haunt cinemas, football matches or even dogtracks.[3]

Seven years before he died, Findlay published an article in the newly-launched *Preachers Quarterly* entitled 'Can we be "Friends of Sinners" and yet separate from them?' He had noticed on a sea voyage the easy associations which Irish Roman Catholic priests could make at the bar and how by sharing drinks they might point some sinners to the Saviour, whereas he stood aloof, afar off, disapproving, uncomfortable. 'I had lost something by becoming a Methodist minister.'

The contemporary Jesus

As we have seen from Flew, the spirituality of this 'school', if such we may call it, was based on the synoptic gospels. The purpose of a series of studies in St Mark's Gospel, published as Manuals of Fellowship over more than a decade, but not extending beyond chapter 6, was to help those who used them, in John Ruskin's words, 'to be present as if in the body at every recorded event in the history of the Redeemer'.[4] To this task, the team brought scholarly gifts of translation and paraphrase (apart from the Gospels, Maltby's paraphrase of Romans 8 is masterly). They believed that each detail of the narrative, rightly understood, could make vivid the events in Palestine long ago and help us to see Jesus as a real person, while 'the manhood of Jesus, steadfastly contemplated, becomes a vista into the nature of God'.[5] There was confidence that we could know Jesus, his mind and times. Bultmann was already overshadowing New Testament scholarship and there was increasing agnosticism about the authentic words of Jesus and Christian origins. The Dead Sea Scrolls had yet to be discovered. Theology was not yet dominating history and although Tyrrell's phrase was often quoted about the 'strange man on the Cross', the Jesus of Maltby and Findlay did not shock and hard sayings could be explained away. T. Francis Glasson attempted this with apocalyptic in *The Second Advent* (1945).

A commentator of the Bultmann school would not write as Maltby did [42] about the Parable of the Sower.[6]

The significance of the cross

As it is the climax of the Synoptic Gospels, the cross was central to these expositors, as we have seen from Flew. He was much influenced by the Anglican Catholic Modernist, A. L. Lilley, who wrote that Christian teaching 'planted the cross at the heart and centre of the prayer-life'.[7] We find God most, not in books, not even in the Book of Books, nor in nature or the human heart, but as we grasp the nettle of suffering with the apostolic words, 'Wherefore I take pleasure in weaknesses, in necessities, in persecutions, in distresses, for Christ's sake; for when I am weak, then am I strong.' As we have mentioned, Flew regarded the Charles Wesley hymn 'Thou shepherd of Israel and mine', as a Christian commentary on Song of Songs 1.7, with its association of the noon where the flock rests with calvary, as 'an unapproachable lyric of the soul'.[8] Calvary is not the place of mourning but 'that happiest place', and the prayer of one who would never leave Christ's flock is

> My spirit to Calvary bear
> To suffer and triumph with thee.

When he was minister at Muswell Hill, Flew on Good Friday would lead worship from the back of the church and base the whole service on one of the

---

42. Even in the imperfect reports which have come down to us of the sayings of Jesus there are scattered words which betray a tender intimacy with growing things and country life. Pure in heart from His youth, he had looked on nature with understanding eyes. We owe much to the mystics, on whom through the visible works of God, His eternal glory breaks; but all their knowledge is as a drop in the ocean compared with the wealth of teaching which Jesus drew from the world around Him. And it would seem that at the time of which we are thinking the analogies of growing seed were much in His mind. Some of His followers were thinking that if only they had the power for twenty-four hours, they would fetch the Kingdom in. They had dreams of a national rising, of victorious armies and scattered enemies. Others looked to see the heavens opened, and the Son of Man coming in the clouds, an end of all debate. Always the same delusion, that force, if there is enough of it, will do the deed! Jesus looks elsewhere for His similitudes. The Son can do nothing but what He sees the Father doing, and the Father's handiwork is all around Him. The parable of the seed growing secretly in the earth that bringeth forth fruit of itself, is conceived with a poet's insight, and it came from a heart full of faith, patience, humility and quiet serenity. Jesus was a tireless Sower, and He always sowed for a harvest. But He knew the harvest He sought could not be forced. Therefore He would neither coerce men nor nag at them, He knew how to sow his seed and how to leave it alone. The message must be left to do its own wooing and the heart to make its own reply. The hireling finds it easy to 'Leave it alone', but that is because he is not eager for the harvest and knows not whether he has sown husks or seed. But Jesus spared Himself nothing in His sowing and already much of the ground proved unfruitful. It gives us pause to see Him stand back to give room and time for the seed to grow, and to hear Him speak of the earth bringing forth fruit of itself, the sower 'knows not how'. There is such faith and humility in that word as might well bring tears to our eyes. He knew indeed that He was not leaving the seed alone. He was leaving it to a thousand ministries, 'a mighty sum of things forever speaking', to the nature of men made for God, to the Spirit who never leaves us and the Love that will not let us go. The most sensitive and vulnerable heart that ever beat on earth was also the most serene. That is the miracle of Jesus. 'He sowed His seed over hill and dale, and on the last bare hill He sowed Himself.'

Source: T. R. and W. R. Maltby, Studies in St Mark, I, Epworth Press 1920, pp. 14–15.

> **43.** It is love of this kind which begins to give us some insight into the love of Christ … A good many years ago I knew a working man in the north of England whose wife, soon after her marriage, drifted into vicious ways and went rapidly from bad to worse. He came home one Sunday evening to find, as he had found a dozen time before, that she had gone on a new debauch. He knew in what condition she would return, after two or three days of a nameless life. He sat down in the cheerless house to look the truth in the face … He made his choice to hold by his wife to the end … She did not mend and died in his house after some years in a shameful condition with his hands spread over her in pity and in prayer to the last.
>
> *Source:* W. R. Maltby, *Christ and His Cross*, Epworth Press 1935, pp. 77f.

Passion hymns of Charles Wesley, with appropriate scriptures and prayers. Maltby gave the Cato lectures in Australia in 1935 and made of them a most beautiful book, *Christ and His Cross*, seeing the atonement as God-in-Christ's betrothal to the human race, his total identification, a synoptic counter to substitutionary theories.

For these men Calvary [43] rather than Pentecost was the heart of the gospel. In 1933 four members of the Oxford Group Movement took part in the Southport Convention. The Movement with its

> **44.** Sometimes, as I read about the Oxford groups, and feel the contagion of their new experience of God, I wonder; is a religion of success and power adequate for the world, or, for that matter for me? This new Oxford movement will only touch the fringe of the problem presented by the uneasy state of the modern Church, the desperate condition of the world, unless not merely Pentecost but Calvary is in the heart of it. The only Pentecost which can really turn the world upside down is the Pentecost that shall follow a new vision of Calvary.
>
> *Source:* J. Alexander Findlay, *What did Jesus Teach?*, Hodder 1933, p. 212.

revival of groups not unlike the class meeting with open confession, and its emphasis on the daily quiet time and listening to God for guidance was to have considerable influence on many Methodists. In the same year, Alec Findlay had written of the inadequacy of the Group in words which could be applied to the Holiness Movement [44], and in a Sheffield Congress booklet, Findlay felt that the values of Methodism at the time of the 1932 union, were not those of Jesus Christ [45].

> **45.** We hear continually of the resources of our Church. He said that the richer you grow, the harder it is to get into the Kingdom.
>
> The first question asked about a minister is, 'Is he an acceptable preacher?' He took it as an axiom that no prophet is acceptable among his own people, and at the end of three years ministry, he was crucified by those to whom he came! We believe – or it would appear that we do – in advertising: 'He would not strive nor cry' and seems to have been chiefly anxious that those who saw his wonderful works should not make them known. I know that such contrasts can be in various ways mitigated. Is it not better to confess that on these matters we have not the mind of Christ?'
>
> *Source:* Alec Findlay, *Jesus the Perfect Man*, Sheffield Congress Booklet (London – undated), p. 4.

There was a hymn of Wesley's [46] which epitomized the spirituality of such as Findlay, certainly in contrast to enthusiastic and noisy heartiness. It is quoted by the Anglo-Catholic sociologist, Kenneth Leech, in his book of spiritual direction, *Soul Friend.*[9] It begins at the second verse of the original, the first, praying for the Christ within, hidden in the heart, being omitted in all editions of the hymn book after 1742.

Flew knew and used ancient prayers of the church, from the early sacramentaries and the Eastern Liturgy of St James. Prayer, for him, is 'the ascent of the mind to God'. In his teaching on prayer, he followed A. L. Lilley, 'that great theologian' closely, not least in his distinction between Christian prayer and

46. Open, Lord, my inward ear,
     And bid my heart rejoice;
     Bid my quiet spirit hear
     Thy comfortable voice;
     Never in the whirlwind found,
     Or where earthquakes rock the place,
     Still and silent is the sound,
     The whisper of thy grace.

     From the world of sin, and noise,
     And hurry I withdraw;
     For the small and inward voice
     I wait with humble awe;
     Silent am I now and still,
     Dare not in thy presence move;
     To my waiting soul reveal
     The secret of thy love.

     Thou didst undertake for me,
     For me to death wast sold;
     Wisdom in a mystery
     Of bleeding love unfold;
     Teach the lesson of thy Cross:
     Let me die with thee to reign;
     All things let me count but loss,
     So I may thee regain.

Source: 1780 Collection, No. 348.

and deeds of kindness, his bearing of the cross long before he was nailed to the wood on Calvary, his suffering when he was rejected and deserted, his bearing of so much obloquy and pain. Thus we see the deep meaning of his prayer in Gethsemane and the final triumph of the Love that will not let us go.

Leslie Weatherhead, as a preacher, always gave as much attention to the conduct of worship as to the sermon. He was a considerable composer of prayers and his card *Ten Minutes a Day* went though countless editions and helped many people to understand that prayer is more than asking. The climax of his devotional writing was *A Private House of Prayer*, which owed something to Teresa of Avila's *The Interior Castle*. Some Methodists, of course, felt that all this was a desertion of the old ways, and believed that prayer, both public and private, should be an uninhibited and spontaneous outpouring of the heart to God, fervent and sometimes noisy, as in the days of the prayer meetings.

For discussion

1. What kind of 'success' should we look for as a result of our Christian witness?

2. In what ways should we be separate in our lifestyle from the majority of people?

3. How would you define liberalism in theology?

4. Why is there now more scepticism about the Jesus of History than in the time of Maltby and Findlay?

5. Read A. N. Wilson's book on *Jesus* (Sinclair Stevenson 1992). What do you think of it?

that of the natural man. 'The natural man prays for visible, material benefits. But the Christian view is that mere man cannot pray at all, and that no desire of his can constitute real prayer. It is God in us who prays. It is our nature, penetrated by the Divine Spirit and assisted by the Divine grace, that is capable of true prayer in the full Christian sense'.[10]

Flew would often in his leading of worship make the prayers meditations on Jesus and the Gospels, leading the congregation to the contemplation of Christ in resistance to temptations, his compassion

16

The Groups

The first half of the twentieth century was the great age of groups, in which Christians banded themselves together to pursue common aims. It was out of such groups that the ecumenical movement sprang, though many of them were not inter-confessional. The pattern was usually the same – a simple rule of life, local meetings with a winter course of study, and the annual Conference at High Leigh or Swanwick. The war and the desire to maintain its camaraderie gave impetus to this movement but in no sense created it, for many of the groups had begun before 1914.

The three most influential movements of this kind in Methodism were the School of Fellowship, held annually at Swanwick, from 1916, of which Maltby, Findlay and Flew were pioneers and which produced the manuals from which I have quoted; the Fellowship of the Kingdom for ministers, founded after the First World War and, in the late 1920s and early 1930s, the Cambridge Groups, pioneered by Harold Beales, the precursors of the University Methodist Societies destined to flourish for thirty years and still extant. They all represented alternatives to the Holiness Movement. They were concerned with Methodism for the future.

The Fellowship of the Kingdom

The Fellowship of the Kingdom, like the Holiness Movement, has been examined by Ian Randall of Spurgeon's College and I am much indebted to his account.[1] It emanated from a group of London ministers somewhat downcast in the time of war and aware that the spiritual life of Methodism was not that of the New Testament. Its watchwords were 'Quest' and 'Crusade', the former implying that Christians were called to be seekers after the truth into which the Holy Spirit leads, not simply those who had recovered a past experience of truth already attained. This rather set Cliff College and the Southport Convention against them. Chadwick declared that he was no longer on a 'Quest' since he had found through the experience of Scriptural Holiness what others were groping for.

The inter-war Conferences from 1920 at Swanwick were more group occasions than dominated by great preachers, though some addresses like those of Boyns, Orchard and Weatherhead were forever memorable. A Quiet Day, or morning, was central and there was an atmosphere of great, though unforced, spiritual intensity during which many found themselves in the presence of God and gave themselves to him in Christ to the regeneration of their ministries. I knew a former Primitive Methodist minister, Phil J. Fisher, minor poet and writer on prayer, who told me that he had stayed up all night after one Conference session renewing his experience of God and giving himself again to Christ. Leslie Weatherhead testified that the Fellowship of the Kingdom had meant more to him than anything else in his ministry. Jesus rather than the Holy Spirit was central, though, as Maltby said, there is something about pooling the honours among the persons of the Godhead. At the first Swanwick Convention a particularly vivid moment was described: 'A Voice began to sound within each man's heart and on a never to be forgotten evening, He Himself, unheralded, was in the midst and spoke his own authentic word. Men had been thinking and speaking of His Cross: and they found Him afresh and mightily.' In 1922, a report in the *Methodist Times* compared Swanwick with the meeting of Jesus and his disciples at the Last Supper: 'The difference between Swanwick and the Upper Room is not one of kind but only of degree.'

There were winter study groups, some of which degenerated into gossip shops, and the high level was not maintained in every ministry. But the Fellowship saved many a minister from loneliness. It delivered from individualism. Ian Randall thinks that the exclusive clericalism of its beginning was a serious limitation. It did not bring lay people into its experience when it was most intense in the inter-war years and did nothing to heal the clerical/lay division, while it reflected the spirituality of the more prosperous south rather than the north and of the towns and suburbs rather than the rural areas. In its heyday it led to a liberal evangelicalism with a recovery of the sacrament of holy communion and an understanding of mystical prayer. In 1922 a thunderstorm and resultant darkness coincided with communion, making real the cry of dereliction amid the darkness of Calvary. The next year, a member testified to the 'great Awe of the real Presence' which fell upon the Conference during 'a silent, wholly silent partaking of the bread and wine'. W. E. Orchard, the Congregationalist Catholic, destined for Rome, was a guest speaker and had great effect. In spite of some connections with the Anglican Evangelical Group Movement, the Fellowship of the Kingdom remained essentially Methodist, concerned with the rehabilitation of the denomination out of which it came. W. E. Sangster, a prominent member, destined for nationwide influence and anxious to save holiness from the evangelical underworld, said in 1936: 'If we are to have a share in reviving the Catholic Church and helping God to use it in saving the world, it will be by our own denomination. Other men will serve it best by working in their Communions. Reunion can look after itself.'

The mysticism of J. A. Chapman

One of the founders, and a minister to whom more attention should be given, was John Arundel (Jack) Chapman. He was a scholar who taught Systematic Theology at both Didsbury and Headingley Colleges. Among much else, he attempted to apprise Methodists of the teaching of Barth and Brunner. His sense of the supernatural came from these rather than from Catholic sources though, like so many, Flew above all, he often quoted Baron von Hügel, the Roman Catholic lay theologian who died in 1925 and whose distinction of the mystical, historical and institutional elements in Christianity became definitive. He insisted that in the end a man can no more be supported by a religion which is not his own than he can by the life-blood flowing through the veins of another.[2] Chapman accepted biblical criticism and felt that it made Jesus more real to us; we could know him better than at any period since his own and a transforming experience of him was never more possible. When he was a young minister walking in London, Chapman had an experience 'of the mystical presence of Jesus and of sudden freedom from doubt, fear and sin'. This helped to draw him away from an attraction to Unitarianism. He saw a new evangelism as 'more inclusive in its recognition that saved and lost were not absolutes and the way of the cross was not the old asceticism but an embracing rather than renouncing of the world'. He was, like others we have mentioned, a preacher of the cross. 'For too long', he said, 'we have been seeking a satisfactory theory of the Atonement when our vital need was a satisfying experience of the Cross.' He was one of the first to go into public houses to smoke his pipe and drink with the men, though his were temperance beverages. 'Dissatisfied with outworn methods,' said a report about him, 'this enterprising minister had cast precedents and even propriety on one side.' (The repudiation of nicotine has made contact between the religious and the man and woman in the street less easy. There are no more 'Woodbine Willies' or Newton Flews who smoke a pipe out of evangelical conviction as well as enjoyment.) Chapman combined evangelicalism and spirituality. He had great faith in Methodism, its doctrines of forgiveness, the Spirit and fellowship and Perfection and he believed that God was about to use it again in the 1930s as one of the instruments of the revival which, together with Weatherhead and Soper as well as the Holiness Movement, he was still expecting. His devotion was based on 'our hymns', 'the Bible in verse'. The hymn-book he used was the one of 1874, the last to be most faithful to the *Collection* of 1780. Some would argue that each hymnbook since has been less helpful to essentially Methodist devotion. The cry must, however, be, not 'back to Wesley', but 'forward from him'.

Chapman became increasingly influenced by the Oxford Groups, their ideal of 'surrender', though perhaps they did not connect it with its deep evangelical root in the forgiveness of sins, and the discipline of the 'Quiet Time'. I have memories of hearing him preach in March 1930 when I was a boy of nine and just before he moved from Didsbury to Headingley. It was a sermon on prayer as 'the practice of the presence of God' the like of which I was not likely to hear again in Methodism for many years. He told of a man who would say the *Te Deum* to himself every morning as he shaved. (Chapman regarded the *Te Deum* as the greatest hymn of the Christian Church.) The sermon would contain some simple and basic teaching about acts of recollection. In the evening, when I was not present, he preached on the cross. I think my father told me that they sang, 'Would Jesus have the sinner die?' It was a great loss when he died in circumstances of deep distress in 1934.

This may account for the passing of his memory. He was subject to spiritual highs – more than once his experience of Christ was renewed – followed by lows. A deep depression led to him throwing himself off a high peak in Derbyshire. This oscillation disturbs, but it is not uncommon for those of intense and mystical experience. The Oxford School of Psychology sees psychosis as an extreme point on a continuum of normal human variation rather than a disease completely different from 'normality', though what leads people from the benign influences of experience to deep depression may depend on traumas in childhood, or some fundamental instability, deep in the unconscious.

Those we have been considering were not the Orchards of Methodism, though Chapman, like many more, recalled his address at Swanwick. The itinerant system would not make it easy for any so inclined, or for Methodist churches to house the mass as Orchard did at the Congregationalist Kings Weigh House. But there were Catholic and sacramental affinities. Chapman endorsed Wesley's attitude to the Lord's Supper in the sermon on 'The Duty of Constant Communion'.

---

47. With the same absolute conviction with which the savage devours his slain foe in order to take his foe's bravery into himself must the Christian take Christ into every fibre of his being to penetrate with the Divine might of his self-sacrifice, every part of his nature and every energy of his life. Only when we have thus taken Christ into the very depths of our being, so that our voice speaks with his tones and our very thoughts are penetrated with his quickening presence, can we be meet instruments in his hand for the salvation of the world he died to redeem.

Source: James Hope Moulton, *The Neglected Sacrament*, Epworth Press 1919, p. 92.

The 'neglected sacrament'

There was published in 1919, after his death by drowning due to enemy action two years earlier, a selection of James Hope Moulton's sermons and addresses, which takes its title from one of them, *The Neglected Sacrament*. This seeks to redress the balance between the eucharist of the Synoptic Gospels and the washing of the disciples' feet found in John's Gospel, which latter, Moulton felt, neglected by the church, was the necessary completion of the breaking of bread and pouring of wine. He thought that the equivalent in 1899 of the mutual foot washing was the Methodist class meeting. He realized, however, that not everyone is able to make group confession, or expose their inmost soul in company. Some need one-to-one encounters. Like Findlay, Moulton was much influenced by the Quaker textual critic and devotional writer, Rendel Harris. The eucharist was not central to his sacramentalism. Yet he has a passage in a communion address [47] intense enough for the most ardent Catholic, though it is reminiscent of his friendship with Sir James Frazer of *The Golden Bough*.

Findlay always interpreted the Lord's Supper by the 'comfortable words', 'Come unto me all ye that labour and are heavy-laden and I will give you rest', quoted in both Zwingli's rite and Cranmer's, who took them from Hermann von Wied, Archbishop Elector of Cologne. They appear in the Church of England Alternative Service Book, 1980. But Findlay too was not a high church sacramentalist. Yet he loved the communion services at Didsbury, possibly because they were held in the old college chapel, which was more like a prayer room and free of ceremonial. And in a *Methodist Recorder* article in June 1934, he wrote:

> The deciding factor will not be our enthusiasm for the propagation of our work or the maintenance of our Church, but our readiness, if need be, to lose our identity in a sacrificial crusade for union and the vindication of the Church, which is his bride and his body.

For discussion

1. 'Now I have found the ground wherein
   Sure my soul's anchor may remain.'
   Is the idea of Christian discipleship as a 'quest' compatible with such assurance?

2. What is the difference between the algebra classes at Cliff College, seized by what was believed to be the descent of the Spirit, and the much quieter but equally intense awareness of the numinous presence of Christ at Fellowship of the Kingdom Conferences?

3. Was Sangster right in thinking that the recovery of holiness within denominations was the right way rather than the direct association of churches in the search for union?

4. Are you able to acknowledge a debt to membership of a group, whether local or national ?

17

Catholics and Protestants

There were, however, Methodists who could not escape the lure of Catholicism. Scholarship after all crossed boundaries. In 1933, at the time of the centenary of the Oxford Movement, R. N. Flew was invited to write an essay for the commemorative symposium edited by N. P. Williams and Charles Harris on *Northern Catholicism*. It is called 'Methodism and the Catholic tradition' and is the final chapter.

Methodist catholicism

Flew discovers three main Catholic notes of Methodism – the passion for holiness, the communion of saints and doctrinal orthodoxy. The first establishes immediate kinship with the original Tractarians. The volumes of Newman's *Parochial and Plain* Sermons start with a sermon on 'Holiness without which no man shall see the Lord'. Flew is soon among the Wesley hymns ('Our hymnbook is our liturgy. It is our liturgy both in public worship and private prayer'). Chiefly from these, he illustrates his contention that, according to Methodists, holiness is offered to all, is centred on the cross, is essential for the success of evangelism and is founded on the great Christian tradition which transcends all ecclesiastical divisions. Wesley made available to men and women out of the common way works from every Christian tradition, not least the Church of Rome.

Under the 'communion of saints' Flew mentions both the class meetings and the holy communion. The Lord's Supper was a 'converting ordinance', 'because the consciousness of personal relationship with God was passed on in the fellowship and often at this Sacrament'. 'The bread of life is the gift of God, but it is broken from hand to hand.' The authentic succession from the first days, as Methodists conceive it, is evangelical rather than historic. The church is the fellowship of Christian personalities, learning the secret of God's personal dealings with them and passing it on to others. It is difficult to see what could be added to this rich spiritual inheritance by the acceptance of the doctrine of the apostolical succession.

Flew adduces 'the full-orbed orthodoxy' of the hymns and the Methodist adherence to the Catholic faith evidenced in William Burt Pope's systematic theology (Later Dom Gregory Dix was to acknowledge privately that this was 'Catholic') and John Scott Lidgett's address to the uniting Conference on the Nicene Creed. He concludes with a coda on Discipline and the hope of complete Methodist dedication to the cause of reunion (in which he was to play a significant part).

The work of Henry Lunn

There was a remarkable if somewhat eccentric Methodist, Sir Henry Lunn (1859–1939). He had been ordained and was for a brief while a medical missionary in India. His mentor was the great Methodist leader Hugh Price Hughes, with whom he organized the valuable conferences for church leaders at Grindelwald in Switzerland. When he resigned from the Methodist ministry, Frederick Temple, the Bishop of London, offered him Anglican ordination, which he refused though, as a layman, he was confirmed by another Bishop of London in 1910. Meanwhile he became for a few years a minister of the Methodist Episcopal Church (Swiss Conference). He regarded himself 'at most a nonconforming member of the Church of England'. He wrote three books of devotion over twenty-two years, *The Love of Jesus* (1911), *Retreats for the Soul* (1913) and *The Secret of the Saints* (1933).[1]

The first is specifically addressed to 'the people called Methodists'. Lunn contrasts the discipline and fervour of the mid-Victorian period with its meetings for prayer and regular fast days with the coldness of the new century. Here we have one of those jeremiads which were to re-echo throughout the Connexion until the onset of the Second World War temporarily drowned them. 'We have deserted our first works and lost our love.' Lunn's solution was to stress the Catholic affinities of Methodism, to go back beyond Aldersgate Street to the Oxford Methodists and the Holy Club. Offices, fasting and frequent communion are his remedies. He provides simple offices for morning and evening, reserving confession for the night – an improvement on Cranmer and the penitential tradition. There is less use of the Psalter than is traditional. He follows Lancelot Andrewes' paraphrase of the Lord's Prayer, some devotions for every day of the week taken from Wesley, Andrewes, and á Kempis and Prayers for the Christian Year with particular concentration on Holy Week. There are the extracts from Wesley's *A Companion for the Altar,* abstracted, of course, from á Kempis, and a selection of the *Hymns on the Lord's Supper.* Lunn prints the whole of the communion service with prayers for use afterwards and guides to Bible study from the American Methodist, J. R. Mott, and to fasting from John Wesley. Archbishop Cosmo Lang, who, though in some aspects prelatical and pompous had an interior life of deep devotion, said in 1930 that he used *The Love of Jesus* constantly.

Retreats for the Soul has less Methodist reference and owes more to the Catholicism of the Counter-Reformation, after the Council of Trent in the middle years of the sixteenth century. It is a book to encourage the practice of withdrawal from the world for periods of silent recollection. After some introductory chapters on needs, history and methods, it consists of spiritual writings, such as the *Preces Privatae* (Private Prayers) of Lancelot Andrewes, the *Spiritual Combat* (Lorenzo Scupoli, 1589) and the *Imitation of Christ* arranged for use on Retreat. There is also a selection of sacred poetry, ranging from St Bernard through the Carolines, the German Mystics, Wesley, Keble and Faber, to Evelyn Underhill. *The Practice of the Presence of God* is included, doubtless to help the return to the kitchen sink when the Retreat is over.

At the end, Lunn gives programmes of four Retreats in which he has shared. Two of them were for Methodists. One, at Swanwick in September 1912, seems to have been very much the kind of Conference-Retreat which is all that talkative Methodism has usually been able to manage; but the other, in June 1913, was for Methodist undergraduates at Oxford and seems to have followed the genuine pattern, though conversation was allowed at meal times and from 11.30 a.m. to noon and from 2 p.m. to 4 p.m. each day, which adds up to a considerable amount.

It is doubtful if Lunn's second volume had much influence in his own communion, though it sold 8,000 copies in all. The word Retreat has been used increasingly in Methodism since about 1952, and there is now a Methodist Retreat Group.

The Secret of the Saints laments further decline in the practice of prayer. A Committee on Corporate Prayer had been set up by the Wesleyan Conference of 1930 and had issued a questionnaire to Superintendent Ministers. Here are some of the replies. 'Prayer,' says one, 'is more a problem than a practice.' Another writes: 'The majority of Methodists have no interest in prayer.' Yet another says: 'I have come to the conclusion that Methodism, as I know it, has lost the desire for social prayer and unlike Mr B. I am both hopeless and helpless.'[2]

Lunn has no difficulty in showing that this is in complete contrast to the experience of the saints of all communions, and he reviews the history of prayer [48] with tremendous insistence that the supreme occasion of corporate prayer is the eucharist and our private devotions should be related to this.

---

48. From the prisons of Imperial Rome; from the solitary hermitages scattered along the banks of the Nile; from caves and castles under the blue skies of Italy and Spain; from the home of the bishop of Geneva on the beautiful shores of the Lake of Annecy; from the torture chambers of the inquisition; from the tower of London, from Bedford jail; from the 'Temples of Silence' in Pennsylvania; from the little room in Aldersgate Street; from Oriel College and Hursley Vicarage there comes an ever-growing stream of testimony to the power of prayer; and an ever-increasing volume of lessons by which Our Lord and His Apostles of every age must answer our cry, 'Teach us to pray'.

Source: Henry Lunn, *The Secret of the Saints*. Heffer 1933, p. 5.

The Secret of the Saints is the most original of Lunn's trilogy, though, as the extensive bibliography shows, it is quarried from almost the whole of Christian Spirituality. After the Introduction there are five chapters: 'The Masters of Meditation'; 'How to Pray'; 'The Art of Meditation'; 'The Discipline of Love'; 'The Vision of God', the last drawing heavily on Kenneth Kirk's Bampton lectures of 1928. Then there are some concluding meditations and Gilbert Shaw's *A Pilgrim's Chapbook* as an appendix. The book aims to be as truly catholic as Wesley's *Christian Library* which is part of its inspiration, though it omits the Puritans.

Lunn has some sympathetic pages on the Oxford Groups, which in their pristine freshness of 1933 were doing much to revive the spiritual life in all communions, by offering the simple method of listening to God in the quietness, in contrast to the overloaded techniques of the mystical manuals, and the agitated repetitious enthusiasms of the old-time prayer meeting. Most spiritually sensitive Methodists found the Groups at this stage of great value and were anxious

to make available the positive insights of the Movement. It was the developing extravagancies in some of the groups, the disdainful attitude to the church, the subjectivism of much of the guidance and the increasing heterodoxy and compromise with extreme political movements of the right which led to disillusion, though we have noted Alec Findlay's warning.

The spirituality of T. S. Gregory

Lunn's spirituality was a development from one aspect of Wesley, but it did not represent popular Methodism and was likely to have more influence outside Methodism than within. There were many other Catholic Methodists among his contemporaries, most notably T. S. Gregory, an Oxford graduate, one of a dynasty which went back to the earliest Methodist preachers, the first of whom was the illiterate we have mentioned who learned to read almost miraculously from a tombstone. 'T.S.' was a great power in the Swanwick Schools of Fellowship. Franciscan type reminiscences of him were long extant in the Circuits he served.

He wrote one of the Fellowship manuals on 'The Compassion of Jesus'. This is of a different genre from the more liberal manuals of the Maltbys and Alec Findlay. T. S. Gregory's cousin, A. S. Gregory, ends his introduction to it with the much quoted words of Albert Schweitzer from *The Quest of the Historical Jesus* [49].

---

49. He comes to us as One unknown, without a name, as of old by the lake-side, He came to those men who knew Him not. He speaks to us the same word: 'Follow thou me!'... And to those who obey Him, whether they be wise or simple, He will reveal himself in the toils, the conflicts, the sufferings, which they shall pass through in His fellowship, and, as an ineffable mystery, they shall know in their own experience who He is.

Source: Albert Schweitzer, *The Quest of the Historical Jesus* [1910]; reissued SCM Press 1981, p. 401.

The manual is a work of mystical genius, in which the Jesus of History, Incarnate, Crucified, Risen Son of God, is seen as 'perpetually born again, everlastingly dying into the life of his friends, so that in the embrace of his compassion' they cannot but feel a glorious liberty 'and own that his are the words of eternal life'. Together with this goes the belief in the church as Christ's mystical body, the theme of a manual written by A. S. Gregory. Kingsley Lloyd wrote '... Christ lived in his church as once he lived in human flesh, the Lamb of God slain from the foundation of the world, still offering himself in his perfect humanity for us men and for our salvation.'[3]

It was out of these convictions that the Methodist Sacramental Fellowship was born. T. S. Gregory devised 'a five year plan' for Methodism, such being then in vogue. It was to make its people more conscious of their Catholic and sacramental heritage. He provided the first draft of a basis for a Methodist Sacramental Fellowship, but, though supported by quotations from Wesley and Brevint, this was rather hard and too inclined to equate disbelief in dogma with sin.

Before the Fellowship was founded in August 1935, T. S. Gregory had become a Roman Catholic, brought to a change of allegiance as he wrote *The Unfinished Universe*, a history of thought. It sees the fundamental difference between the finished, mechanistic universe in which man is the measure of all things and human life the end, and the incomplete universe, the mystery of a purpose not yet consummated, life and history open with something to be done and God, not far-off, removed, impassible, but involved in all suffering and action with a chosen community which, for Gregory, is the Roman Catholic Church. This is an original and surprising thesis. The book had some prestigious reviews.

Gregory had an influential career as a Roman Catholic layman and never needed to abandon his devotion to the Wesley hymns on which he wrote a Lent book in 1966, *According to Your Faith*. A fine and deeply moving study, it was unfortunate in that it came out in the heyday of radical theology when, for many, tradition was at a discount and the hymns no longer spoke to their condition.

The Methodist Sacramental Fellowship

Gregory's defection did not help the nascent Fellowship, which endured a campaign of opposition. It was vindicated by the Conference of 1938 after a moving speech by Dr J. E. Rattenbury, a famed missioner whom no one could accuse of being an encassocked romanizer. The aims of the Fellowship were: the reaffirmation of the faith of the historic creeds, the restoration of sacramental devotion which proclaims the wholeness of faith and that which unites Christians, and the corporate reunion of believers. Wesley's spirituality is, as we have seen, ecumenical, of the earliest centuries as well as of the Reformation and the eighteenth century, and the Fellowship sought to encourage charity towards other communions and knowledge of their treasures. Its members are bound by a daily discipline of offices, specially composed and revised over the decades.

From the beginning the Sacramental Fellowship, unlike the Fellowship of the Kingdom, was a partnership of ministers and lay people, the latter outnumbering the former by two to one in the first membership. In 1950, Donald Soper became President of the Fellowship, bringing his liberal theology, social evangelism and dedication to the Sermon on the Mount, to a deep sacramental devotion. Soper had founded the Order of Christian Witness in 1947, which was to hold large campaigns in innumerable centres for many years. They always ended with a eucharist, a 'converting ordinance' in which those who had been won for Christ pledged themselves along with the campaigners. As President of the Conference, in 1953, Soper held afternoon eucharists instead of preaching 'rallies', followed by open air meetings, with opportunity for hecklers as at Tower Hill or in Hyde Park.

The devotion of A.E. Whitham

The first President of the Methodist Sacramental Fellowship was A. E. Whitham, who died, somewhat prematurely, in 1938. An unnamed correspondent wrote of him: 'There was much about him of the troubadour and not a little of the Franciscan. There was in him a beautiful blend of goodness and gaiety. He was one of the gayest and most seriously religious persons I have ever met, and how he yearned to enter ever more deeply into the secret of the saints.'[4]

Whitham's sermons and articles, collected into volumes only after his death, are elegant pieces, devotional meditations, for the most part of great insight, imagination and beauty. They are thoroughly sacramental and show how the masters of Catholic spirituality have become part of Whitham's Methodist soul [50]. He tells of a vow he made during the war that if he were spared he would strive for reconciliation with every enemy. 'Then I looked round to find my enemy. I had none among the nations – I was not a patriot of the imbecile order. I had not even a family relation I could call an enemy. But I had one, the Roman Catholic Church, which for me included High Church and Eastern Church. I had no fellowship with it: I had sought none. Here then was my business.'[5]

He then discovered that the large majority of the lovers of Jesus through the ages were on the side of 'the enemy'. 'It seemed a cynical thought that so many were so far astray, pasturing on poisoned herbs. I determined to read their best theology and devotional literature.'[6]

And here we make an unexpected discovery. The person to whom Whitham went for guidance in Catholic theology and devotion was Samuel Chadwick, whom we have mentioned as leader of the Holiness Movement. 'Few people', says Whitham, 'knew how wide a reader that stout apostle of Protestantism was, or how heartily he loved Catholic devotional manuals. He once confessed to me he always had a Catholic book of devotion in constant use on his table.'[7]

Chadwick's biographer provides further evidence of this. It may well have been the intensity of their prayers which, like Wesley and Lopez, drew Chadwick to the Catholics. His one great regret was that he had not prayed more. He revelled in the evangelicals, George Muller and Hudson Taylor, because they were men of prayer. But he confessed that if he had not been a Methodist, he would have been a Roman Catholic and that if the Lord permitted him to come into this world again and he could choose his sphere he would be the abbot of a monastery. He loved the season of Lent. 'Lent requires sacrifice, devotion and prayer. These things may take worthless forms and then they are worthless, but they stand for deep spiritual necessities of the soul. That is why the six weeks of Lent should be so ordered as to give opportunity for concentration of heart and mind upon the Cross and Passion of Our Lord Jesus Christ.'[8]

---

50. . . . I thought I was treading the streets of the Holy City, pottering about like a tourist. In my wandering I came upon the museum of that city of our dreams. I went in, and a courteous attendant conducted me round. There was some old armour there much bruised with battle. Many things were conspicuous by their absence. I saw nothing of Alexander's nor of Napoleon's. There was no Pope's ring, nor even the ink bottle that Luther is said to have thrown at the devil, nor Wesley's seal and keys, nor the first minutes of Conference, nor the last (I was sorry about that because my name was in it). I saw a widow's mite and the feather of a little bird, I saw some swaddling clothes, a hammer, and three nails, and a few thorns. I saw a bit of a fishing net and the broken oar of a boat. I saw a sponge that had once been dipped in vinegar, and a small piece of silver. But I cannot enumerate all I saw, nor describe all I felt. Whilst I was turning over a common drinking cup which had a very honourable place I whispered to the attendant, 'Have you not got a towel and basin among your collection?' 'No!' he said, 'not here; you see they are in constant use.'

Source: A.E.Whitham, *The Discipline and Culture of the Spiritual Life*, Hodder 1938, pp. 4of.

'You, too, can be a saint'

This shows that it is a mistake to look for Catholic devotional influences simply among obvious high church people and pioneers of ecumenism. Serious Christianity and deep devotion to Christ may unite those of different traditions across the barriers of hierarchical system and ceremonial. W. E. Sangster's book *The Pure in Heart* (1954) is astonishingly Catholic in its exempla. Earlier, he had sought in *The Path to Perfection* to restate the Methodist doctrine in a more popular form than that of Flew's *The Idea of Perfection in Christian Theology*. In 1957, he wrote one of a series of pamphlets, 'You can be a Saint'. He sought to redeem the word from its misuse, though surprisingly he does not include the common opinion that a saint is one who, however admirable, is not equipped to deal with the realities of worldly life. In the New Testament, claims Sangster, a saint 'is one who has received the Holy Spirit and in whom Christ is being formed afresh'. Some would say rather that the primary meaning is one who belongs to the community of the baptized, the new Israel of Christ's believers, who already live in the end-time when God's kingly rule is breaking into the affairs of the world. The saints, Sangster says, are few, but they could be many, for sanctity, that is, being a real Christian, is possible to all, in spite of those who say that we can never advance beyond forgiveness, or those who make false claims. The world needs saints. It is interesting that writing in *The Independent* newspaper in the late 1980s, Lord Rees-Mogg in an article which feared that civilization might end by the middle of next century, thought that only saints could prevent this.

Sangster goes on to say that sanctity is a gift of God. It may be attained by believing that this is what God intends. He means to make us like his Son. We should imaginatively contemplate ourselves in Christ. This opens our hearts to all the resources of heaven and makes it possible for us to witness the miracle of ourselves truly changed. Sanctity is retained by the 'moment-by-moment' life of attention to God in prayer and obedience. Saints may be given some awareness that they are growing in grace. They can test this negatively by the extent to which they disown love of money and worldly ambition, and positively as they bear suffering and disillusionment and hatred is banished from their hearts. But saints think less and less of themselves and their own goodness. Other people discern it in them. They never announce it; indeed the more they advance in holiness the more they are conscious of their distance from God.

For discussion

1. How do you account for the fact that, from the beginning of Methodism there was fear of Rome, yet this was accompanied by a great attraction and kinship beneath the surface?

2. Why is the practice of prayer so difficult for the ordinary person?

3. 'A beautiful blend of goodness and gaity'. Would you agree that is as important to have a joyful spirit as it is to do good works?

4. What do you think are the characteristics shown by saints? Do you know any 'saints'?

18

Methodism and Protestantism

The inter-war years were the time of distinguished conversions to Catholicism, such as those of G. K. Chesterton and Evelyn Waugh, and some Methodists looked towards it too. The Sacramental Fellowship was founded; there were a few defections to Rome, apart from T. S. Gregory, some temporary. It was succeeded by a revival of Protestantism, fostered by Newton Flew, whose catholic understanding was unquestioned, but who had a considerable knowledge of continental theology and sent out travelling scholars from Wesley House, Cambridge, to Germany. Thus Methodists kept pace with Barth, whom Chapman had earlier expounded, and the renowned Lutheran scholarship of Gordon Rupp and Philip Watson was born, the latter also devoting himself to translations, notably the second volume of Nygren's *Agape and Eros* and of his other works.

Another strong influence was the German church struggle. This killed forever Methodist fascination with the Oxford Group and Buchmanism, which was unable to discern the evils of Hitler or resist pagan myths of blood and race. Biblical theology was in the ascendant, deduced from the belief that the Bible was the unified word of God and that literary criticism could but show it as the foundation of the faith of the creeds. The Bible declares that sin runs like a scarlet thread through human life and we are redeemed through the act of God in Christ to whom the whole of scripture bears witness. A Lutheran such as Franz Hildebrandt, who had been Niemöller's curate and a colleague of Dietrich Bonhoeffer, became a Methodist rather than an Anglican and found a Lutheran succession in the Aldersgate experience and the Wesley hymns.[1]

Revival of Methodist hymnody

There was much celebration of Methodist hymnody at this time and a spate of books. A. S. Gregory wrote *Praises with Understanding* in 1936. Outstanding were Bernard, Lord Manning's *The Hymns of Wesley and Watts* (1942) and J. E. Rattenbury's *The Evangelical Doctrines of Charles Wesley's Hymns* (1941), to be followed in 1948 by his volume on *The Eucharistic Hymns of John and Charles Wesley*. Flew's *The Hymns of Charles Wesley: A Study of their Structure* (1953)) is brief but luminous. Alec Findlay regarded hymns as his 'second string' after the New Testament and his brother George published *Christ's Standard Bearer: A Study of the Hymns of Charles Wesley* in 1956. But even in the late 1940s, some of the younger generation were finding the hymns difficult and not expressive of an intelligible faith. They spoke in a language which was not in the concepts of the life they lived or the world they knew.

The climax of the work on hymnody was the publication in 1983 of Franz Hildebrandt's and Oliver Beckerlegge's magnificent edition of the 1780 *Collection of Hymns for the Use of the People called Methodists*. This not only annotates the hymns, providing scriptural references, but has a superb and comprehensive introduction with a fine theological section by Hildebrandt, and bibliography and indices. Unfortunately, when once living outbursts of faith receive such scholarly attention, they have often become museum pieces. The edition will not restore Wesley to the Methodist people, while, as a footnote points out, the disappearance of the Authorized Version of the scriptures and the Book of Common Prayer makes many of Wesley's references meaningless. For those hearing and using new translations, the hymns are no longer, as Chapman and Rattenbury asserted, 'the Bible in verse'.

The then young scholar, A. Raymond George, whose main contribution to Methodism was to be in liturgy, gave the Femley-Hartley lecture in 1953, *Communion with God in the New Testament*, of which Michael Ramsey among others thought highly. It is a most thorough examination of all relevant passages, written with cool, scholarly precision, out of deep and unquestioning faith. George uses Heiler's distinction between prophetic and mystical prayer and believes that New Testament prayer is mostly to be understood as the former, though there is some synthesis as in the prayer of Gethsemane. The mystical spirituality of the New Testament is a development of the Jewish-Christian tradition and not an importation from paganism. George criticizes Kenneth Kirk's book *The Vision of God* and does not find evidence to suggest that to see God is the goal of the Christian life. The beatitude that this is the reward of the pure in heart is without echo in the first three Gospels. Communion, though it is used but nineteen times in the New Testament, is most richly expressive of our relation to God through Christ.

Methodist scholarship

The 1940s were the age of Kenneth Kirk, Bishop of Oxford, and Dom Gregory Dix in the Church of England. To their attempts to restate the high Catholic doctrine of orders and apostolic succession in such works as *The Apostolic Ministry* (1946) and the pamphlet *Catholicity* (1947), Methodists and Free Churchmen generally were eager to oppose the

splendour and true catholicity of their own heritage. They did this in *The Catholicity of Protestantism* edited by R. Newton Flew and Rupert E. Davies in 1950. Meanwhile, Philip Watson's Fernley-Hartley lecture on Luther's theology, *Let God be God* (1947) and the works of Gordon Rupp, *Studies in the Making of the English Protestant Tradition, Luther's Progress to the Diet of Worms* and *The Righteousness of God* placed Methodists firmly in the tradition of Protestant scholarship. Irvonwy Morgan in several works and I myself in *Puritan Devotion* (1957) contributed to the large movement of scholarship, much of it from the United States, for the rehabilitation of Puritanism. Philip Watson expressed the mood in his 'reader of instruction and devotion', *The Message of the Wesleys* [51].

In 1965, Gordon Rupp gave some broadcast talks

---

51. It has more than once been alleged that Protestantism has produced 'no devotional literature' – a charge which on any showing is at least highly exaggerated. But naturally everything depends on what 'devotional literature' is supposed to be. If it is literature designed to foster 'the life of God in the soul of man' – to borrow with Wesley the title of a famous work of Puritan edification – then Protestantism has produced such literature in abundance and in large variety. Protestantism not only gave the Bible to the common man in his own tongue, but its scholars and theologians gave him commentaries on it, to assist him in applying its teaching to his life, and its preachers and teachers supplied him with printed sermons, tracts, and treatises on the spiritual life. They wrote and published journals describing their own spiritual pilgrimage for the help and encouragement of others; they gave personal spiritual counsel in letters; and they produced collections of hymns setting forth the doctrines of the faith and describing the varieties of spiritual experience. Such literature was available and was widely used, both by individuals privately and by family and other groups, through generation after generation of Protestants till the widespread decline of piety in recent times.

Source: Philip Watson, *The Message of the Wesleys*, Epworth Press 1964, pp. xi–xiv.

on the Christian conflict in history, published as *Principalities and Powers*, which restated the Methodist 'optimism of grace' and 'the special coherence and combination of our doctrines. To justification by faith, which is the beginning and groundwork of salvation, to the hope of perfect love, Wesley joined his teaching on the use of the law and on the work and witness of the Holy Spirit.'[2] There is great confidence, shared by many others, that Methodism 'like a silken glove' has been 'the most flexible instrument for evangelism in Christian history' and, the implication is, that it could be again [52].

---

52. The Arminianism of Wesley had little to do with the academic writings of Arminius . . . It maintained the biblical, Protestant diagnosis of the depths of our human tragedy, which we only realize when we confront the Righteousness of God. But it set 'total grace' over and against 'total sinfulness'; it breathed an optimism of Grace, which changed the whole mood and temper of English Christianity and nerved it for the battle against the giant evils of the coming industrial age.

Not only the occasion, but the results of separation (from the Church of England) have to be considered. When we have defended the sincerity of John Wesley and when we have repudiated the discussion in Anglo-Catholic terms, we have still to face the question whether there has not been in consequence a moving away from the deep elements in historical Christian continuity, which gave original Methodism a depth and stability not always evident in later days.

Source: Gordon Rupp, *Methodism in Relation to Protestant Tradition*, Epworth Press 1951, pp. 20, 23.

Conversations on unity

This confidence prevailed throughout the 1950s. The Anglican-Methodist conversations about unity which began in 1955 presupposed that Anglican-Methodist unity might lead to the conversion of England. W. F. Lofthouse in an essay written in the 1950s on 'Charles Wesley' in the first volume of Davies and Rupp (eds), *A History of the Methodist Church in Great Britain* declared that 'with the prayer-book in the form to which the larger part of Methodists were accustomed for a century, and with the modification in the hymns which all Methodists now accept, an atmosphere might be created, with a common *lex orandi* (law of praying) and *lex credendi* (law of believing), which could make union in some form possible and desirable to all'.[3]

Liturgical reform

But both Anglicans and Methodists were beginning the process of liturgical revision. Cranmer was no longer uniting the Church of England and discoveries of ancient liturgies were making his Protestant rite unacceptable for some. *The Apostolic Tradition* of Hippolytus (c. 215) bedazzled liturgists and Cranmer was charged with mutilating the great thanksgiving of tradition. And, as we have seen, the Wesley hymns were beginning to lose their appeal. Anglican-Methodist unity failed, ironically in part because the remarkable reforms of the Second Vatican Council gave Anglo-Catholics the hope of their long-desired union with Rome, which many of them felt would be impeded by closer relations with the Methodists. They were wrong and the Council did as much for Roman Catholic-Methodist rapprochement as for Roman-Anglican. There had always been beneath the fears and suspicions a fellow-feeling, due to Anglican discrimination against both, and to the Methodist spirituality of perfect love and its expression in hymns which included devotion congenial to Roman Cathlics on the Passion of Christ and the eucharist.

For discussion

1. If this is an unfinished universe, should not the chosen people, fellow-workers and sufferers with God, be an 'open' community, not exclusive and with intolerance as a virtue?

2. 'Not I, but Christ liveth in me'. Are others able to say that as well as Paul? Are you?

3. It has been said that the word Protestant really means the same as the word Catholic. Do you agree?

19

Radical Spirituality

The 1960s were the age of radical theology in which many lost confidence in Orthodox Christianity and in traditional methods of spirituality. Methodists like others were affected by secular Christianity, 'Christianity without religion', Jesus as 'the man for others', by such people as Dietrich Bonhoeffer [53] and John Robinson [54]. There was great longing for spiritual freedom, for prayer not as an ascetic discipline but as a share in the sufferings of a suffering God. In some instances the freedom desired was freedom from God, at least the God of orthodox theology, which, some believed, Jesus made possible. Some satirized this with the old jibe against Catholic modernists, 'There is no God and Jesus is his Son.'

Leslie Weatherhead wrote *The Christian Agnostic* in 1966. It helped many waverers, not least some people faithful to the church, whose orthodoxy was

---

53. We cannot be honest unless we recognize that we have to live in the world *etsi deus non daretur*. And this is just what we do recognize – before God! God himself compels us to recognize it. So our coming of age leads us to a true recognition of our situation before God. God would have us know that we must live as men who manage our lives without him. The God who is with us is the God who forsakes us (Mark 15.34).The God who lets us live in the world without the working hypothesis of God is the God before whom we stand continually. Before God and with God we live without God. God lets himself be pushed out of the world on to the cross. He is weak and powerless in the world, and that is precisely the way, the only way, in which he is with us and helps us . . .

Here is the decisive difference between Christianity and all religions. Man's religiosity makes him look in his distress to the power of God in the world: God is the *deus ex machina*. The Bible directs man to God's powerlessness and suffering; only the suffering God can help. To that extent we may say that the development towards the world's coming of age outlined above, which has done away with a false conception of God, opens up a way of seeing the God of the Bible, who wins power and space in the world by his weakness. This will probably be the starting-point for our 'worldly interpretation'.

Source: Dietrich Bonhoeffer, *Letters and Papers from Prison*, The Enlarged Edition, SCM Press 1971, pp. 360f.

---

54. When Tillich speaks of God in 'depth', he is speaking of 'the infinite and inexhaustible depth and ground of all being', of our ultimate concern, of what we take seriously without reservation . . .

What Tillich is meaning by God is the exact opposite of any *deus ex machina*, a supernatural Being to whom one can turn away from the world and who can be relied upon to intervene from without. God is not 'out there'. He is in Bonhoeffer's words 'the "beyond" in the midst of our life', a depth of reality reached 'not on the borders of life but at its centre', not by any flight of the alone to the alone, but, in Kierkegaard's fine phrase, by 'a deeper immersion in existence'. For the word 'God' denotes the ultimate depth of all our being, the creative ground and meaning of all our existence.

Source: John A. T. Robinson, *Honest to God*, SCM Press 1963, pp. 46f.

not as secure and unquestioning as it appeared. It was a brave book but lacked the theological toughness of the radical theologians and was disappointingly eclectic, flirting with reincarnation and other notions and subjective in its judgments. I said at the time that the book is mistitled. It is agnostic only about the claims of orthodox Christianity, the doctrine of the Trinity and the like. It gives free rein to insights from other faiths and offers a pick and mix *gnosticism*. Yet there shines out from it a love of Jesus and a longing to help ordinary people to a living faith.

The eucharist retained its hold – though not for Weatherhead – and increased in Methodism. It carried the message of food for the hungry, the fellowship meal and the self-giving of Christ for the world. A sermon of Chapman's on an aspect of the sacrament has a footnote pointing out that it was preached at a service 'at the close of which there was Holy Communion'. The 1975 Sunday Service established in Methodism what should, of course, have been apparent from Cranmer, that word and sacrament belong together. The communion is now rarely a closing rite or an after-meeting.

A strong strain of Methodist devotion has been prayer for the overseas districts represented by the annual prayer manual, to the value of which there was much testimony, missionaries at difficult stages and in great loneliness receiving strength on the day they were prayed for at home. The balance now shifted from evangelism supported by prayer to aid. It was more Christian to provide food and medicine for needy people than to preach gospel sermons. Provision for life before death was more important that the promise of life after.

Political spirituality

There was from the 1960s to the abolition of apartheid in South Africa a strong movement which identified spirituality and political freedom and like the World Council of Churches supported freedom fighters against oppressive regimes. Some of its adherents added justice to peace when they gave the 'kiss' at the eucharist. They were not pacifists and although some of them had been first inspired by Donald Soper, they did not follow him to this extent, nor were so openly socialist. Colin Morris's *Include Me Out*, product, partly, of his work with Kenneth Kaunda in Zambia, was a testament. And they often kept an arcane, unadvertised, spiritual discipline. They cried publicly for justice; they prayed, as Jesus counselled, in secret.

This was succeeded by a revival of evangelicalism, though of a type after the Lausanne Conference of 1968, not indifferent to social needs. Pentecostalism revived world-wide and Methodists shared it, notably Cliff College, but it did not originate in Methodism and is not a Methodist phenomenon, or even solely Christian. It in no sense swept the denomination. But at some services Methodists spoke in tongues and believed that this was a manifestation of the Spirit, the receipt of which was a special mark of grace. That this was a gift of Pentecost was contested by William Arthur, as we have seen, as by the modern poet, W. H. Auden.[1]

For discussion

1. How do you understand Bonhoeffer's belief that man has 'come of age'?

2. Do you find 'ground of being' a more helpful concept of God than the personal?

3. What do you understand by 'secular Christianity' or 'religionless Christianity'?

4. Would you find 'Creator, Redeemer, Sustainer' a more helpful description of the Trinity than the more traditional 'Father, Son, Holy Spirit'?

20

Methodism and the Vogue for Spirituality

There has been vast writing on spirituality since the 1960s, much of it a restatement of orthodoxy and by Roman Catholics. I attempted to describe some of it in a chapter of my *The Life of the Spirit in the World of Today*, a book which also gives account of the radical spirituality of its time and the undermining by some of Christian theology [55].[1]

> 55. The one clear conclusion [of the radicalism of the 1960s] is simply this: ours is an age of empiricism and no philosophic forms or practices will be accepted unless they are seen to work. No declaration about God, or the world, or prayer will be heeded unless it coheres with what men actually know of life as they live it. No symbol or tradition of the past will be honoured unless it reverberates in our experience now.
>
> *Source*: Gordon S. Wakefield, *The Life of the Spirit in the World of Today*, Epworth Press 1969, p. 159.

The spirituality of J. Neville Ward

Since 1967, there has been one Methodist spiritual writer of genius, J. Neville Ward (1915–1992). A minister and the son of a minister, he was never lured from Methodism or from its Epworth Press. He probably believed that a change of denomination would not necessarily be a homecoming to Catholic faith. But his teaching was Catholic and he was no unstinting admirer of Wesley, or propagator of 'our doctrines'. Of philosophic mind influenced by D. Z.

Phillips and *The Concept of Payer* and steeped in literature, he wrote readily and well. He was highly cultured, inspired and consoled by music, fond of good food and drink. He once said that he became more 'trad' every day, but was a thinker of creative originality. His first book, *The Use of Praying*, freed people from guilt about prayer, delivered them from the tyranny of request-response, and led them through the dark night and the dry seasons. Prayer for him was the extension of the eucharist into seven weekly attempts at living. It is an exercise towards loving, a reflection in depth as to what God and life and love are in the Christian tradition [56]. His next book, *Five for Sorrow, Ten for Joy* was on the rosary: following the Anglican Austin Farrer, he regarded it as the 'heaven-sent aid' to prayer. *Friday Afternoon* was a profound meditation on the Passion. His influence may have been greater beyond Methodism than within it, though he brought help to many in his own communion.[2]

> 56. Prayer is always to be understood in terms of the religious tradition in which it is offered. A Buddhist monk at prayer is doing what is understood by prayer in the Buddhist tradition. A Christian at prayer is doing what is regarded as prayer in the Christian religion, if it is the instructed and adult Christian in him who is praying and not some lazy or neurotic self; that is to say, he is affirming, expressing, deepening his dependence on God and his desire for God's kingdom.
>
> *Source:* J. Neville Ward, *The Use of Praying*, Epworth Press 1967, pp. 15f.

In 1972, the then President of Conference, Harry Morton, appointed a Commission to report on spirituality. It did so to the Conference of 1974. It was born of a desire to recover Methodist discipline and rule of life in terms appropriate to the times and by enriching distinctive Methodism with the experience of other traditions. There was particular concern for the ordained ministry, often disheartened, and undergoing peculiar problems of the age from the tension of work in the inner cities and housing estates to pressures on marriage. Outside the Commission, Harry Morton and I undertook some investigations into the Anglican Oratory of the Good Shepherd, an order with vows regularly renewed, but with its ministry exercised in parishes and colleges. We had thoughts of something similar in Methodism but nothing came of it.

Distinguishing features of Methodist spirituality

The Commission singled out certain features of Methodist spirituality from the variety and differences of its life, such as the expectations still aroused by preaching, the sense of family, community service and social activity, pragmatism that is a church organization which meets the needs of the time rather than based on ideology, lay participation and leadership, advance in the Christian life and the quest for unity. The principal recommendations were:

1. The voluntary acceptance of a rule of life by those who desire it. This should include minimum obligations of prayer and worship, responsible use of personal resources, the right use of time and training in Christian understanding, declaring ourselves as Christians and sharing the faith with other people. Keepers of the rule should meet together regularly to work out its implications and provide mutual encouragement, direction and oversight.
2. The encouragement and formation of religious communities.
3. Participation of the Methodist church in existing retreat houses.
4. These houses could be centres of spiritual life for Methodism. Ministers and their families could spend periods there, possibly sabbaticals, write and conduct retreats and direct postal courses.

The Report hardly caused a spiritual revolution in Methodism. It may not have been propagated as it ought once it had been presented to Conference. The community ideal was tried out in several places, but encountered difficulties of personal relationships and ecumenically. The 1970s was a decade in which many community experiments were tried. Some have survived without having a wide-ranging effect. Some, like the Farncombe Community, have not outlived their instigators, though they were of service in the decades of their life, providing retreat in an ordered community and spiritual direction. The Fellowship of Prayer is still in existence.

Ecumenical spirituality

Mary Holliday, formed in the school of Dorothy Farrar and Maltby's Deaconess Order, and later Head of the Farncombe Community, influential in ecumenical spirituality, has claimed that the Commission has borne fruit 'quietly and slowly'. The Retreat Group evolved from ecumenical beginnings in the late 1960s and has a steady existence. Methodist spirituality has become ecumenical with Catholic tendencies. Many have benefited from the Spiritual Exercises of Ignatius Loyola, that flexible and adaptable method of meditation, which in many churches has renewed ministries and proved invaluable for lay people. But it is Ignatius who is in vogue, not Richard Baxter or Russell Maltby. This may be due to its amalgamation with Myers Briggs psychology with its Jungian premises, which many find attractive, though some authorities like Rowan Williams and Kenneth Leech are opposed to it. There has also been the influence of the community at Taizé in France and use of its forms of prayer.

The other developments are in evangelicalism, and these, one suspects, are more widespread. Spring Harvest and the meetings of the Methodist Easter People are well-attended. The Bible teaching, aided academically by post-modernism is, in some ways, Puritan, certainly uninfluenced by more radical scholarship, and choruses have supplemented and to some extent displaced the traditional hymns. Words are repeated sounds rather than conveyors of theology, and bodily movement, swaying, hands uplifted or clapping is the accompaniment. There is a feeling that traditional worship has become dull and lifeless

and transatlantic importations have brought 'enthusiasm' and a transendence of rationality. One may ask in matters of spirituality 'Where is Methodism to be found?'

For discussion

1. How would you describe prayer?

2. Is the 'request-response' understanding of prayer a 'tyranny' in spite of the teaching of Jesus?

3. What would be your definition of 'spirituality'?

21

Restatements beyond Methodism

The provocative fact is that Wesley's 'grand depositum', belief in perfection and desire for holiness, are apparent in writings from various communions with no reference to Wesley or Methodism at all.

A. D. Lindsay was a Scottish philosopher, son of a notable and ecumenical Scottish theologian, Master of Balliol College, Oxford, unsuccessful parliamentary candidate, and afterwards founder of Keele University. He distinguished two moralities: that of 'my station and its duties', which is necessary for the right ordering of human affairs, and the 'morality of grace', which does not stand on its rights, shows compassion beyond demands, is, in fact, the morality of the Sermon on the Mount. Dorothy Emmet, interpreting Lindsay, thinks that there are two kinds of the morality of grace, which he fused, Wordsworth's 'little, nameless, unremembered acts of kindness and of love' and 'the heroic, sacrificial morality of the saint'.[1] Both Lindsay's moralities are needed. The morality of codes, of reciprocal rights and obligations, becomes rigorous and power-seeking unless the morality of grace, creative and imaginative, comes into it. Yet if society tried to live by the morality of grace alone it would fall into anarchy. The point for us is that the morality of grace, the Sermon on the Mount, is a call to perfection. This is needed as an 'operative ideal', though it is never fully realized or realizable. But it is as necessary for society as for the individual to believe that there is held out to us a call to perfection, a height of spontaneous, self-forgetful love which ever beckons us on and without which our life would become pedestrian and compromised. Otherwise we should never transcend the market place.

Holiness is for all

Donald Nicholl, who died at the beginning of May 1997, was a Roman Catholic layman, also an academic, Professor at Keele and California and Rector of the Ecumenical Institute for Theological Research at Tantur, near Bethlehem. He was catholic very much in the sense of Wesley's catholic spirit. In 1981, his book on *Holiness* was published, and a second edition came out in 1987.

This is not from the world of academe, or book learning, but from Nicholl's experience of human life in many continents. It insists that holiness is for all, not for some few spiritually gifted, and it draws its examples from many faiths, an amazing variety of sources from many periods of human history and many cultures. An Orthodox saint keeps company with a Muslim Iman, a mediaeval Jew, a Tibetan Buddhist, a Japanese psychiatrist, a victim of Auschwitz, or some person Nicholl has known or encountered. The quest is ecumenical in a sense wider than Wesley's in that, like Bernanos' country priest, he finds grace everywhere. Yet Holiness must draw us into the Holy One. Without a trace of Christian imperialism, the supreme instance is in the Christ of the incarnation and Calvary. Nicholl believed in him as the Way, the Truth and the Life, but believed that the unconditional love of God accepted in Christ opens up for us the treasures of other religions. The Passion, the one final sacrifice for the whole creation, is inescapable. There is one, unacknowledged and slightly inaccurate, quotation from a Wesley hymn, 'the wounds which all my sorrows heal' from 'With glorious clouds encompassed round'.[2] There is subscription to the Christian doctrine of the Trinity, with which Weatherhead and others, like David Francis, have been unhappy, but which the Wesleys affirmed totally. 'According to that teaching ultimate reality is Three-Personed, the perfect union of Father, Son and Holy Spirit. For the human person holiness means sharing even more fully in that divine friendship.'[3] The eucharist is also inescapable, its universality glimpsed in the sharing of food or tokens of food in other faiths.

Holiness is a gift. To the dying thief on the cross it was granted immediately, 'today', without any preparation. But we should put ourselves in the way of it. It comes from connatural, not simply supernatural knowledge, in accordance with nature and at home in the universe. It grows from the performance of menial tasks, making tea for others and doing the duty nearest. Manual work, contrary to Aristotle, seems essential to sanctity (Christ was a carpenter). It is a turning towards the light, but not without cost. (A Methodist New Testament teacher said to a student that the gospel is not self-fulfilment, but self denial.) Holiness 'always costs not less than everything'.

'God longs for every one of his creatures to be holy.' He is not a severe taskmaster but a gentle Father. He 'loves mankind not only with a father's love, but with the love of a mother for the child of her womb'.[4] Frustrations may not be impediments to holiness but conditions for it as with the Curé d'Ars. Yet there must be a longing commensurate with God's for us.

Responsibility for our bodies is of the greatest importance, for our tongues, our sexual members, our ears and all our parts. We are even responsible for the corpse that we leave behind. We are representatives of mankind. And we never know what knowledge will help us in human service. Whatever we seek to learn or do must be with a sense of responsibility.

Stillness is necessary, the need to stop and be silent at times. We may hurry or talk God out of our lives, even in the way we eat our food. We need to learn the sabbath rest, sometimes to be detached from those habits we think are wholly good, or those spiritual exercises which come to dominate our lives. The Jesus prayer may help us to pray without ceasing so that prayer descends from the mind to the heart.

Daily life should be a spiritual exercise, but we must not let 'the trivial round, the common task' save us from concerns with the wider issues of society. One may need to abandon one's present position in society, good and satisfying as it is, for the sake of the poor, as Mother Teresa did.

We need companions, friendship, community, a soul-friend, 'someone who loves you so much that he will never allow you to stray from the path of holiness without both rebuking and encouraging you'.[5] (The friend may often be 'she'.) The family and the church in some forms are essential. There are times, though, when one needs to be with the Holy One alone. Whitehead was not totally misguided when he said 'Religion is what the individual does with his own solitariness.' The Methodist report on spirituality recognized the vocation of those called to be hermits.

The most searching and awesome chapter of *Holiness* is on suffering; self-sacrifice. No one can become holy without being plunged into the mystery of suffering. Both St Paul and Mohammed thought that groaning was the state of the creation and, said

---

57. Consequently if we ask ourselves, 'What is the very worst thing that could happen to me in this life?' the answer would have to be the complete opposite of the answer that worldly folk give. The worst thing that could happened to me in this life is that I should always have perfect health, always have interesting work and plenty of money to buy things and take holidays, and also manage somehow never to be brought into contact with suffering. If that were to happen to me I should be turned into a monster, something unnatural, incapable of compassion for other creatures. To be cut off from suffering is ultimately to be cut off from joy.

Source: Donald Nicholl, *Holiness*, Darton, Longman and Todd 1981, pp. 145f.

Mohammed, one of the names of God. Nicholl refers to C. S. Lewis whose book *The Problem of Pain* seemed superficial, even to himself, when he had suffered the grief of his wife's death from cancer. Suffering is not a problem but a mystery. It takes the initiative out of our own hands. It may, as with Job, draw us ever deeper into the presence of God and of one another. Strangely, joy and suffering are not opposites [57]. The Jews sang in the train to Auschwitz about the day when they would feast upon Leviathan. The Hasidim danced in praise of God in the streets of Warsaw before they were massacred. 'To be cut off from suffering is ultimately to be cut off from joy.'[6] But the sufferer like the unblemished lamb of the Jewish sacrifice must be pure, innocent, unselfconscious. Vicarious, redemptive suffering must always be of the innocent, the 'not-harming'.

This is a brief and inadequate summary of a book full of detail and illustrations, which describes the full scope of holiness and how it has been attained. Methodists should not be sour because the main reason for their existence has been interpreted for our time by one not of their own. Methodist spirituality may be restated by those with little knowledge of its history and expression in its own people. We may learn it anew in a wider context, not only of Christianity but of world faiths. As represented by such as Donald Nicholl, the Church of Rome could yet become a home for all who seek it. One fears that old rigorisms and excess of ultra-montane zeal may make this impossible. And liberal theology, by no means dead, is not incompatible with deep Christian devotion.[7]

Meanwhile, Methodists must be as open as Wesley to every manifestation of holiness, of perfect love of God and neighbour, and seek both the loss and discovery of self in Christ and in care for humankind.

For discussion

1. Why have Flew and Sangster been ignored and Wesley's 'grand depositum' of Christian perfection been more faithfully taught by those outside modern Methodism?

2. To what extent must our ecumenism henceforth include other faiths as well as other Christian denominations?

3. Is fundamentalism the enemy world-wide of all religions?

4. Have Methodists invested too much in 'our hymns', so that when they pass from fashion we are much impoverished in our devotion and in our offer to the world?

5. What is your definition of 'holiness'?

Glossary

ANGLICAN Not in general use before the nineteenth century. It refers particularly to the Church of England, the established state form of Christianity, and its distinctive order and spirituality and includes churches all over the world which originate from that church.

ANTEPAST A poetic expression, found in Wesley hymns, meaning a foretaste or something to whet the appetite.

ANTI-NOMIANISM Literally 'against the law'. Its extreme form is condemned by Paul in Romans 6: 'shall we continue in sin that grace may abound?' It so emphasizes God's grace and the futility of works that the moral behaviour of Christians does not seem to matter. It was a serious option in the seventeenth and eighteenth centuries.

ARMINIANISM From Jacob Arminius (1560–1609) who opposed Calvin's teaching on predestination and believed that all could be saved, not simply the elect. The will was free to choose or reject salvation and it was possible to fall from grace. This strongly influenced Wesley. In the seventeenth century it had political overtones in England. Arminians were more royalist and Anglican than Puritan.

ATONEMENT The reconciliation (at-one-ment) between God and humankind which was achieved by his Son Jesus Christ. Over the centuries different theories have arisen which try to show how this is possible. Some focus on the sacrificial nature of Christ's death on the cross, some on his victory over evil, and others on the 'moral' force of God's love at work through Christ. No one theory explains this reconciliation completely, but each contributes something to our understanding.

AUGUSTINIAN Augustine (354–430) was perhaps the most famous of the early Church Fathers and of immense influence both on Catholics and Protestants. His *Confessions* tell the remarkable story of his conversion, which, though very personal, has been something of a model to later Christians. From his own experience he came to believe that humanity's original sin could be countered only by the grace of God. A winsome and attractive man, with a genius for friendship and a profound understanding of the Divine love, he became somewhat soured by controversy on this and other matters. He is not to be confused with Augustine, the first Archbishop of Canterbury who lived in the sixth century.

CATECHUMEN One who is receiving catechesis or instruction in the Christian faith, being prepared for membership.

CATHOLIC 'The holy Church throughout all the world'. Also the authentic church which bears the marks of apostolic Christianity. The word describes those Christians who set great store by this rather than by personal experience. It should not be confined to those who obey the Pope.

CHARISMATIC From the Greek word *charism* meaning grace. The term 'charismatic' refers specifically to the movement in the church that represents the gifts of the Spirit. Charismatic worship is found particularly in Pentecostal churches though it has become widespread among many Christian denominations. Its main characteristics are the absence of normal liturgies, a high degree of congregational participation, stress on corporate extempore prayer, singing and movement, prophecy and speaking in tongues.

CONNEXION The national network of Methodist churches, comprising local churches, circuits and districts, linked together in progressively larger units, under the government of the annual Conference.

CONTEMPLATION The method of prayer in which the mind is at rest, thinking no longer dominates, the imagination is inactive, words are few. There is a simple resting in God without effort, a looking towards him, and absorption in his love. Classically, it has been seen as a stage of advance beyond meditation, but for some it may be the beginning of prayer. It is not confined to Christianity, but found in all religions.

ECUMENISM/ECUMENICAL The term originates from the Greek *oikumene* meaning the whole inhabited world. It describes the movement, particularly in the twentieth century, which seeks the unity of all Christian people, though whether this should be organic or co-operative provokes some differences.

ENTHUSIASM Literally inspiration, or God possession. It has been used, particularly in Wesley's day, for movements of religious extremism. It was a term of abuse, denoting a fanatic.

EUCHARIST Literally 'thanksgiving'. A name given to the sacrament of holy communion as early as the second century, which is now the standard ecumenical term, being less extreme than 'Mass' on the one hand or 'Lord 's Supper' or the 'breaking of bread' on the other.

EVANGELICAL A loose term having a number of different meanings. In the nineteenth century it described an informal group within the Church of England, many of its members lay, who were known for their piety and laid great stress on the need for personal conversion and the spreading of the gospel. Today it refers to Christians who emphasize the importance of the doctrine of justification, evangelistic outreach and the authority of scripture.

EXTEMPOREE A sermon or prayer given without help of notes, sometimes impromptu.

FUNDAMENTALISTS Fundamentalists believe in the verbal inspiration of scripture and therefore its supremacy as the inerrant word of God. Consequently, they insist on the literal interpretation of the Bible.

GRACE From the Greek *charis* meaning charm, gracefulness or graciousness. In Christian theology, it refers to God's love, unmerited and free, which longs for the reconciliation of sinners and is always beforehand in taking the initiative and bringing to repentance. There is, however, a subsidiary meaning, of the virtue received particularly in the sacraments. Hence Newman can write of 'a higher gift than grace' which on the former meaning would be absurd if not blasphemous.

HOMILIES Sermons written by Cranmer and others to be read by those clergy incapable of composing their own. They are masterpieces of Protestant doctrine.

LIBERALISM IN THEOLOGY Openness to new thought and scientific discovery. Confidence in historical criticism of the Bible as leading to deeper knowledge of the truth, devotion to the humanity of Jesus and concern with ethics, Christian behaviour, more than with dogma.

LITURGY Literally, the work (of the people). It often means any formal service, whether the set forms of an authorized prayer book, or a freer order which follows certain principles, includes the vital elements of worship and is the custom of a particular denomination. In the Eastern Orthodox Church it is the name for the eucharist.

LITURGICAL MOVEMENT Originating in France in the nineteenth century and spreading throughout Europe across all denominations, this arose from a general desire to renew the worship of the church. It stressed the importance of the sacraments and the observance of the Christian year but also placed renewed emphasis on preaching. Christian worship is the union of word and sacrament and the celebrants are the whole congregation, not those set apart to preside.

MEDITATION Prayer with the mind, often inspired by passages of scripture or other texts which are applied to the situation of the praying individual or group. It involves the imagination, what is called 'composition of place', picturing the scene or a whole story, being present as in the body at recorded events. It should lead to a sense of the presence of God and a resolution about one's life. Preaching is often a form of it.

MYSTICISM A very long tradition, not confined to Christianity which, put very simply, seeks for an immediacy of union with God, though this is often achieved only after long and disciplined effort, self-denial, renunciation of worldly interest and loves and an experience of desolation such as that of Christ on the cross. When that is attained there is unspeakable joy and peace, and the whole world is given back in all its glory. St John of the Cross, who experienced the agonies of the dark night of the sense and soul was, none the less, the greatest lyrical poet in the Spanish language, while many mystics have been men and women of action.

OFFICE From the Latin Officium, duty. In liturgy it refers to the keeping of certain hours of the day for ordered devotions based on the Psalms. In the monasteries there were eight of these. Cranmer reduced them to morning and evening prayer.

OXFORD GROUP Founded by Frank Buchmann, it had great success in the 1930s with its emphasis on guidance through the Quiet Time, listening to God, group confession, surrender to Divine demands and from 1938 'Moral Rearmament'. It lost influence through its naive simplicity and its softness towards Hitler.

OXFORD MOVEMENT Begun in the Church of England in 1833 under the leadership of eminent Oxford Divines, it sought to free the church from being merely an instrument of the state by reaffirming its divine origins and Catholicity. It led to a high view of the clerical vocation and in time to an increase of ceremonial and the adoption of Roman Catholic practices. It had immense influence and until recently, when it has become much divided, was in its less extreme forms, the leading movement in the English Church.

PIETISM A movement which began in seventeenth-century Germany in reaction against Lutheran rigidity about justification by faith alone and its belief that, though forgiven, one remains a sinner. It was influenced by Puritanism and also found an English form in Methodism. It practised prayer through the love of God and formed conventicles, or small groups. It produced hymn writers some of whom Wesley translated.

PREDESTINATION The belief that out of humanity, totally depraved, God in his mercy chooses some for salvation. He made this choice before ever they were born, before the foundation of the world, and they, in spite of lapses, will endure to the end, though their reward may be diminished if they have committed certain transgressions. 'Double predestination' means that God chooses some to be damned. Wesley was vehemently opposed to it, stressing that God's love is for all. It did give courage and confidence to those who were assured of their election and saved them from the depressions and self-searchings of revivalists, if converts were few and the world continued in its evil ways. Coleridge said that it was comforting to the individual, cruel to the race.

PROTESTANT Adhering to the Reformation of the sixteenth century, but also by that allegiance 'an appeal to God in Christ, Holy Scripture and the Primitive Church against all degeneration and apostasy'. Up to the middle of the seventeenth century, Protestant was understood by those who professed it to include the designation of Catholic.

PREVENIENT GRACE God's grace anticipates our own response to it. This is an argument for infant baptism. God loves us before we have faith. 'While we were yet sinners Christ died for us.'

PURITANS Those who wished for the reformation of the English church to go beyond the settlement under Elizabeth I. They were mostly Calvinists, though of varying degrees. They felt that the Book of Common Prayer was still too Catholic, though they did not all of them object to set forms and in some ways their understanding of the eucharistic sacrifice could be more catholic than Cranmer's. The keeping of the sabbath was central to their spirituality as was the family conceived of as a church. They were not the kill-joys of caricature, though after 1640 they became divided into many parties and sects. They became nonconformists, dissenters under Charles II and were much deprived and intermittently persecuted, so that Wesley, whose parents had turned away from nonconformity to the Church of England, came to sympathize with them and admire their fortitiude.

SANCTIFICATION The continuing of God's work in the heart of a Christian following conversion. As a process of growth in holiness it marked a real change in a person's character and life.

TAIZÉ The religious community near Cluny in France which began with a group of Protestant pastors. It has exercised a wide influence on liturgy and worship and is well known for its music and chants.

THEURGY Magic though by the agency of good spirits.

For Further Reading

Spirituality in general

Dupré, Louis and Saliers, Don E. (eds), *Christian Spirituality: Post-Reformation and Modern*, SCM Press, London and Crossroad, New York 1989
  Sets Methodism in context and has an important section on twentieth–century trajectories
Jones, Cheslyn, Wainwright, Geoffrey and Yarnold, Edward (eds), *The Study of Spirituality*, SPCK 1986
Knox, Ronald A., *Enthusiasm*, OUP 1950
Rupp, E. Gordon, *Religion in England 1688–1791*, OUP 1986
Wakefield, Gordon (ed), *A Dictionary of Christian Spirituality*, SCM Press and Westminster Press 1983

Methodism in general

Bucke, E. S. (ed), *A History of American Methodism*, 3 vols, Abingdon 1964
Davies, Rupert E., George, A. Raymond and Rupp, E. Gordon (eds), *A History of the Methodist Church in Great Britain*, 4 vols, Epworth Press 1965–88
Davies, Rupert E., *Methodism*, 2nd revd edn Epworth Press 1985
Langford, Thomas A., *Methodist Theology,* Epworth Press 1998
Rack, Henry D., *The Future of John Wesley's Methodism*, Lutterworth Press 1965
Rupp, Gordon, *Principalities and Powers*, Epworth Press 1952
Tabraham, Barrie, *The Making of Methodism*, Epworth Press 1995
Thompson, W. J., Workman H. B. and Earys, G. (eds), *A New History of Methodism*, 2 vols, Hodder 1909
Turner, J. Munsey, *Conflict and Reconciliation*, Epworth Press 1985
Turner, J. Munsey, *Modern Methodism in England 1932–1998,* Epworth Press 1998

John and Charles Wesley

Baker, Frank, *Charles Wesley as revealed by his letters*, Epworth Press 1948

Gill, F. C., *Charles Wesley: The First Methodist*, Lutterworth Press 1964

Green, Vivien H. H., *The Young Mr Wesley*, Arnold 1961

Green, Vivien H. H., *John Wesley*, Nelson 1964

Heizenrater, Richard P., *The Elusive Mr Wesley*, 2 vols, Abingdon 1984

Outler, Albert C., *John Wesley: Selected Works*, OUP 1964
    An anthology with a fine introduction

Rack, Henry D., *Reasonable Enthusiast: John Wesley and the Rise of Methodism*, 2nd edn, Epworth Press 1992. The definitive life

Schmidt, Martin, *John Wesley: A Theological Biography*, 2 vols, Epworth Press 1962, 1973

Vickers, John A., *Charles Wesley*, Foundery Press 1990

Wakefield, Gordon S., *John Wesley*, Foundery Press 1989

Wiseman, F. L., *Charles Wesley: Evangelist and Poet*, Epworth Press 1933

Methodist spirituality and worship

Allchin, A. M. (ed), *We Belong to One Another*, Epworth Press 1965

Bowmer, John C., *The Sacrament of the Lord's Supper in Early Methodism*, Dacre Press 1951

Bowmer, John C., *The Lord's Supper in Methodism 1791–1960*, Epworth Press 1961

Campbell, Ted A., *John Wesley and Christian Antiquity*, Kingswood Books 1991

Dutton, W. E., *John Wesley in Company with High Churchmen*, London 1869

Dutton, W. E., *The Eucharistic Manuals of John and Charles Wesley*, London 1871

Flew, R. Newton, *The Idea of Perfection in Christian Theology*, OUP 1934

Gill, F. C., *John Wesley's Prayers*, Epworth Press 1951

Gregory, T. S., *According to Your Faith*, Epworth Press 1966

Hodges, H. A and Allchin, A. M., *A Rapture of Praise*, Hodder 1966

Lindstrom, Harald, *Wesley and Sanctification*, Epworth Press 1950

Osborn, George, *Poetical Works of John and Charles Wesley*, 13 vols, Wesleyan Methodist Publishing House 1868–1872

Tucker, Karen Westerfield (ed), *The Sunday Service of the Methodists*, Kingswood 1996

Wakefield, Gordon S., *An Outline of Christian Worship*, T & T Clark 1998

Spiritual texts influential studies

Arthur, William, *The Tongue of Fire*, London 1856; reissued Epworth Press 1956

Baxter, Richard, *The Saints Everlasting Rest* [1650] ed John Wilkinson, Epworth Press 1962

Butler, Cuthbert, *Western Mysticism*, Constable 1951

Chapman, J.A., *The Supernatural Life*, Epworth Press 1934

Constable, Giles, *Three Studies in Medieval Religious and Social Thought*, CUP 1995

Findlay, J. A., *Jesus and His Parables*, Epworth Press 1950

Ford, David F. and Stamps, Dennis L., *Essentials of Christian Community*, T & T Clark 1996

George, A. Raymond, *Communion with God in the New Testament*, Epworth Press 1953

Hindmarsh, B., *John Newton and English Evangelical Religion*, Clarendon Press 1996

Law, William, *A Serious Call to a Devout and Holy Life* [1728], many editions including J. M. Dent 1906

Lunn, Henry, *The Love of Jesus*, Hodder 1908

Lunn, Henry, *Retreats for the Soul*, Hodder 1913

Lunn, Henry, *The Secret of the Saints*, W. Heffer, Cambridge 1933

Maltby, W.R., *Christ and His Cross*, Epworth Press 1935

Moulton, J. H., *A Neglected Sacrament*, Epworth Press 1919

Nicholl, Donald, *Holiness*, Darton, Longman and Todd 1981,1987,1996

Nuttall, G. F., *The Puritan Spirit*, Epworth Press 1966

Nuttall, G. F., *The Holy Spirit in Puritan Faith and Experience*, Blackwell 1947 and Chicago 1992

Sangster, W. E., *The Path to Perfection*, Hodder 1943

Sangster, W. E., *The Pure in Heart*, Epworth Press 1954

Wakefield, Gordon S., *The Life of the Spirit in the World of Today*, Macmillan, New York and Epworth Press 1969

Ward, J. Neville, *The Use of Praying*, Epworth Press 1967

Weatherhead, Leslie D., *A Private House of Prayer*, Hodder 1958

Weatherhead, Leslie D., *The Christian Agnostic*, Hodder 1966

Whitham, A. E., *The Discipline and Culture of the Spiritual Life: A Memorial Volume compiled from his Writings*, Hodder 1938

Hymns

Bett, Henry, *The Hymns of Methodism in their Literary Relations*, 3rd edn Epworth Press 1945

Flew R., Newton, *The Hymns of Charles Wesley: A Study of their Structure*, Epworth Press 1953

Gregory, A.S., *Praises with Understanding*, Epworth Press 1938

Hildebrandt, Franz and Beckerlegge, O. A., with the assistance of Dale, James, *A Collection of Hymns for the Use of the People called Methodists*, The Works of John Wesley vol. 7, OUP 1983

Hymns and Psalms, Methodist Publishing House 1983

Manning, Bernard L., *The Hymns of Wesley and Watts*, Epworth Press 1942

Rattenbury, J. E., *The Evangelical Doctrines of Charles Wesley's Hymns*, Epworth Press 1941

Rattenbury, J. E., *The Eucharistic Hymns of John and Charles Wesley*, Epworth Press 1948

Watson, J. R., *The English Hymn*, Clarendon Press 1997

Worthies

Brash, W. Bardsley, *Love and Life. The Story of J. Denholm Brash* by his Son, Kelly 1913

Clarke, Adam, *A Memoir of Joseph Entwistle* by his Son, Mason 1848

Coley, Samuel, *The Life of the Revd Thomas Collins*, London 1896

Dunning, Norman G., *Samuel Chadwick*, Epworth Press 1933

Frost, Brian, *Goodwill on Fire: the Life of Donald Soper*, Hodder 1996

Nettleton, Joseph, *John Hunt*, London undated *c.* 1900

Sangster, Paul, *Dr Sangster*, Epworth Press 1962

Travell, John, *Doctor of Souls: Leslie D. Weatherhead (1893–1976)*, Lutterworth Press 1999

Tyerman, Luke, *Praying William*, Mason 1857

Vickers, J. A. (ed), *Wisdom and Wit. An Anthology from the Writings of Gordon Rupp*, Methodist Publishing House undated

Wakefield, Gordon S., *Robert Newton Flew*, Epworth Press 1971

Wakefield, Gordon S., *T. S. Gregory*, Teamprint, Loughborough 1999

Wilkinson, J. T., *William Clowes*, Epworth Press 1951

Wilkinson, J. T, *Hugh Bourne*, Epworth Press 1952

Articles and pamphlets

Andrews, J. H. B., 'The Rise of the Bible Christians', *The Preacher's Quarterly*, March 1965

Barratt, T. H., 'The Lord's Supper in Early Methodism', *The London Quarterly Review*, July 1923

Beckerlegge, O. A., 'The Sacrament of the Lord's Supper', *London Quarterly and Holborn Review*, October 1964

Bett, Henry, 'The Origins of the Class Meeting', Wesley Historical Society Proceedings, 1931, pp. 41ff.

J. A. Findlay, 'Can we be "Friends of Sinners" and yet separate from them?', *The Preacher's Quarterly*, December 1954

George, A. Raymond, 'Private Devotion in the Methodist Tradition', *Studia Liturgica*, Vol. II, No. 3, September 1963 p. 233

Gregory, T. S., *They Shall See God*, Manuals of Fellowship, Epworth Press 1926

Gregory, T. S., *The Compassion of Jesus*, Manuals of Fellowship, Epworth Press 1929

Maltby, T. R. and W. R, *Studies in St Mark 1–4*, Manuals of Fellowship, Epworth Press 1920ff.

Newton, John A., 'Methodism and the Puritans', Dr Williams' Library lecture 1964

Rupp, Gordon, 'Methodism and the Protestant Tradition', Epworth Press 1951

Rupp, Gordon, 'A Devotion of Rapture in English Puritanism' in Knox, R.Buick (ed), *Reformation, Conformity and Dissent*, Epworth Press 1997, pp. 115ff.

Wakefield, Gordon, 'Methodist Union: Youthful Memories, Adult Assessment and Future Hopes', *Epworth Review*, May 1982, p. 30

Notes

Introduction

1. A. D. Lindsay, *Karl Marx's Capital*, OUP 1931, p. 52.
2. Richard H. Rogers, 'A Post-Modern Church: Theological Reflections on Ecclesiology and Social Theory' in David F. Ford and Dennis L. Stamps (eds), *Essentials of Christian Community*, T & T Clark 1996, pp. 179–95.
3. Alexander Knox, *Remains IV*, London 1834, p. 282.

1 Before 1738

1. See Henry Bett, *Wesley Historical Society Proceedings* 1931, pp. 41ff.
2. A phrase from Hymn 282 in *Hymns and Psalms*.
3. Helen White, *English Devotional Literature*, Madison 1931, p. 81. See also Giles Constable, *Three Studies in Medieval and Social Thought*, CUP 1995, pp. 239–42.
4. Cf. Barrie Tabraham, *The Making of Methodism*, Epworth Press 1995, p. 10.
5. Martin Schmidt, *John Wesley: A Theological Biography*, Epworth Press 1962, p. 10.
6. See V. H. H. Green, *The Young Mr Wesley*, Arnold 1961, p. 256. Jeremy Taylor (1631–67) is the quintessential Anglican Divine. See Richard Askew, *Muskets and Altars*, Mowbray 1997.
7. See Thorvold Kallstad, *John Wesley and the Bible: A Psychological Study*, Stockholm 1974, pp. 74ff.
8. William Law, *A Serious Call to a Devout and Holy Life*, Dent 1908, p. 318.
9. William Law, *Works*, 1893, Vol. V, pp. 183ff. Cf. Daniel Defoe, *A Tour through the Whole Island of Great Britain*, Penguin 1986, p. 209, for a similar use of the word 'catholic'.
10. V. H. H. Green, *The Young Mr Wesley*, p. 83.

11. Albert C. Outler, *John Wesley*, OUP 1964, pp. 99,100.
12. Macarius, *Homilies* ed. A. J. Mason, 1921, pp. 15, 21. See the important discussions in Outler, *John Wesley*, p. 31 and H. A. Hodges and A. M. Allchin, *A Rapture of Praise*, Hodder 1996, pp. 188–200.
13. Wesley, *Works*, standard edition ed Thomas Jackson, John Mason 1829–31, Vol. X, p. 484. 'It is interesting to note the quality in Ephraim which particularly attracts him' (A. M. Allchin in *We Belong to One Another*, Epworth Press 1965, p. 68).
14. A. G. Mortimort in A. G. Mortimort (ed), *The Church at Prayer: The Liturgy of Time*, Chapman 1986.
15. Sebastian Brock, *The Luminous Eye: The Spiritual World Vision of St Ephrem*, CIIS, Rome 1985. See also Brock in Gordon S. Wakefield (ed), *A Dictionary of Christian Spirituality*, SCM Press 1983, pp. 134ff. See also Gordon S. Wakefield, 'John Wesley and Ephraim Syrus' to be published in *Hugoye*, a new Journal of Syriac Studies accessible on the internet.
16. Gerald O'Collins, *Second Journey*, Villa Books 1979.

2 Rapture and Order: 'Our Hymns' and 'Our Discipline'

1. See Franz Hildebrandt and O. A. Beckerlegge, with the assistance of James Dale, *A Collection of Hymns for the Use of the People called Methodists*, OUP 1983.
2. J. E. Rattenbury, *The Evangelical Doctrines of Charles Wesley's Hymns*, Epworth Press 1941.
3. Donald Davie, Introduction to *A New Oxford Book of Christian Verse*, OUP 1981.
4. Hildebrandt and Beckerlegge , *A Collection of Hymns*, No. 9; abbreviated as No. 325 in the *Methodist Hymn Book*, 1933. Cf. the hymn 'Open, Lord, my inward ear' quoted above, p. 66.

5. For the full list see Hildebrandt and Beckerlegge, *A Collection of Hymns*, Appendix H, p. 765. Cf. the section on Methodism in Gordon S. Wakefield, *An Outline of Christian Worship*, T & T Clark 1998, pp. 137f.

6. Ronald Knox, *Enthusiasm*, OUP 1950, p. 432.

7. Sheridan Gilley in Eamon Duffy (ed), *Challoner and his Church*, Darton, Longman and Todd 1981, pp. 107–9.

3 The Means of Grace: Meditation and Mysticism

1. John Wesley, *Minutes of the Methodist Conference*, 1812 edition, p. 17.

2. John Booty in E. Rozanne Elder (ed), *The Roots of the Modern Christian Tradition*, II, Cistercian Publications 1984, pp. 200–28.

3. My own imitation of Joseph Hall.

4. I am indebted to the Revd Gordon Mursell, whose section on Hall for his forthcoming book on English Spirituality I have read and discussed with him.

5. I have used the edition edited and abridged by John T. Wilkinson, Epworth Press 1962.

6. *Hymns and Psalms*, Methodist Publishing House 1983, No. 47.

7. John Telford, *Wesley's Veterans*, London 1912–14. At least one Jesuit was denied consolations for a similar period.

8. For Wesley and Mysticism see Outler, *John Wesley*, OUP 1964 and Hodges and Allchin, *A Rapture of Praise*, Hodder 1966; also Jean Orcibal 'The Theological Originality of John Wesley' in Davies, George and Rupp (eds), *A History of the Methodist Church in Great Britain*, Vol. 1; Hasso Jaeger, *Le Mystique and Les Mystiques*, Brussels 1965; T. Kallstad, *John Wesley and the Bible*, Stockholm 1974, pp. 160–180 and the Wesley chapters in R. A. Knox, *Enthusiasm*, OUP 1950.

9. R. A. Knox, *Enthusiasm*, pp. 432 ff.

10. John Fletcher, *Works*, I, New York 1854, p. 236. Cf. Orcibal, 'The Theological Originality of John Wesley', p. 96.

11. R. Newton Flew, *The Hymns of Charles Wesley*, Epworth Press 1953, pp. 70ff.

12. Henry Bett, *The Hymns of Methodism*, Epworth Press 1920, pp. 60–70.

4 The Means of Grace: The Lord's Supper

1. For this section I have drawn on my chapter in Martin Dudley (ed), *Like a Two-Edged Sword*, Canterbury Press 1995, pp. 139–160.

2. *Hymns on the Lord's Supper*, No. 21. The hymns can be found in Rattenbury, *The Eucharistic Hymns of John and Charles Wesley*, Epworth Press 1948, pp. 195–249. There is also a facsimile edition of *Hymns on the Lord's Supper*, published by The Charles Wesley Society, Madison, NJ 1995.

3. *Hymns on the Lord's Supper*, No. 5.

4. Ibid.

5. Geoffrey Wainwright, *Eucharist and Eschatology*, Epworth Press 1971, p. 152. See also Geoffrey Wainwright, 'Taste and See' in *For Our Salvation: Two Approaches to the Work of Christ*, Eerdmans/SPCK 1997, pp. 36–44.

6. Geoffrey Wainwright, *Doxology*, Epworth Press 1979, pp. 198–217.

5 Other Means of Grace

1. L. F. Church, *More About the Early Methodist People*, Epworth Press 1949, pp. 274 ff.

6 Perfect Love

1. B. Hindmarsh, *John Newton and English Evangelical Religion*, OUP 1996, p. 239.

2. *1780 Collection*, No. 364.

3. Hindmarsh, *John Newton*, pp. 138 ff.

4. Ronald Knox, *Enthusiasm*, pp. 452 ff.

5. *1780 Collection*, No. 379.

6. A. M. Allchin, *We Belong to One Another*, Epworth Press 1965, p. 56.

7 The Social Gospel

1. R. W. Dale, *The Evangelical Revival and Other Sermons*, Hodder 1883, pp. 1–40.

2. I owe much for the illustrations here to the lectures of Dr J. D. Walsh of Jesus College, Oxford.

3. See J. M. Turner, *Conflict and Reconciliation*, Epworth Press 1985, p. 52. Cf. Flew, *The Idea of Perfection in Christian Theology*, OUP 1934, p. 339.

4. E. P. Thompson, *The Making of the English Working Class*, Penguin 1968, p. 338.
5. See Donald Davie, *A Gathered Church*, Routledge 1978, pp. 45–47.
6. Turner, *Conflict and Reconciliation*, p. 52.

8 Communion with God

1. Thomas Collins, cited in Samuel Coley, *The Life of the Revd Thomas Collins*, London 1896, pp. 44f.
2. Coley, *Life of Thomas Collins*, p. 185.
3. Ibid., pp. 186ff.
4. Ibid., p. 130.
5. Cuthbert Butler, *Western Mysticism* (Second Edition with Afterthoughts), Constable 1926.
6. Coley, *Life of Thomas Collins*, p. 135.
7. Missionary work was perilous throughout the nineteenth century. See the story of the heroic United Free Church missionaries to Africa and China in O. A. Beckerlegge, *The United Methodist Free Churches*, Epworth Press 1957, pp. 89f.
8. Joseph Nettleton, *John Hunt*, London, undated, p. 27.
9. Unacknowledged citation by N. Allen Birtwhistle in Davies, George and Rupp (eds), *A History of the Methodist Church in Great Britain*, Vol. 3, p. 19.

9 The Developing Church Consciousness

1. See T. H. Barratt, 'The Lord's Supper in Early Methodism' in *London Quarterly Review*, July 1923. Cf. J. C. Bowmer, *The Lord's Supper in Methodism 1799–1960*, Epworth Press 1961, p. 22.
2. Luke Tyerman, *Praying William*, John Mason 1857.
3. O. A. Beckerlegge, 'The Sacrament of the Lord's Supper' in *London Quarterly and Holborn Review*, October 1964.
4. E.g. W. E. Dutton, *John Wesley in Company with High Churchmen*, London 1869 and *The Eucharistic Manuals of John and Charles Wesley*, London 1871.
5. See Gordon S. Wakefield, ch. 12 in Geoffrey Rowell (ed), *Tradition Renewed*, Darton, Longman and Todd 1986, pp. 185–98.
6. Ibid., p. 190.
7. Adam Clarke, *Memoir of the Revd Joseph Entwistle*, Mason 1848, p. 239.
8. Joseph Sutcliffe, *A Treatise on the Universal Spread of the Gospel. The Glorious Millennium and the Second Coming of Christ*, Doncaster 1798. For Sutcliffe see Kenneth C. G. Newport, *Methodists and the Millennium*, Bulletin of the John Rylands University Library of Manchester, Vol. 78, No. 1, Spring 1996, pp. 109–12. Sutcliffe writes in the aftermath of the French Revolution, and by diligent calculations from Daniel and Revelation in particular, expects the millennium around 1865. Newport shows that such expectations are to be found among the early Methodists, even the Wesleys and Fletcher of Madeley.
9. See the opening essay in John H. S. Kent, *The Age of Disunity*, Epworth Press 1966.
10. J. H. B. Andrews, 'The Rise of the Bible Christians' in *The Preachers Quarterly*, March 1965, p. 58.
11. Coley, *Life of Thomas Collins*, pp. 8–9.

10 Revivalism

1. For an account of camp meetings see E. S. Bucke (ed), *A History of American Methodism*, Abingdon 1964, Vol. I, particularly pp. 507–23; also many references to Lorenzo Dow.
2. Ibid., pp. 513–14. The young man became a pioneer Methodist minister in the Ohio Valley.
3. Ibid., p. 631.
4. Cf. N. H. Snaith in the *Methodist Recorder*, May 1957; W. E. Farndale, *The Secret of Mow Cop: A New Appraisal of the Origins of Primitive Methodism*, Epworth Press 1950, p. 29.
5. J. T. Wilkinson, *Hugh Bourne*, Epworth Press 1952 and *William Clowes*, Epworth Press 1951.
6. G. F. Nuttall, *The Puritan Spirit*, Epworth Press 1967, pp. 204–13. Originally published in *Friends Quarterly*.
7. Wilkinson, *Hugh Bourne*, p. 53.
8. G. F. Nuttall, *The Holy Spirit in Puritan Faith and Experience*, Blackwell 1947, pp. 13–14.
9. Coley, *Life of Thomas Collins*, p. 285.
10. For a remarkable story of the prayers of a Durham miner in perfect liturgical form, quoted by J. A. Findlay, see Leslie D. Weatherhead, *The Christian Agnostic*, Hodder 1965, pp. 98–99.
11. Hubert Northcott, *The Venture of Prayer*, SPCK 1962, p. 44.
12. William Arthur, *The Tongue of Fire*, London 1856, p. 97.
13. Ibid., p. 87
14. Timothy L. Smith in Bucke (ed), *A History of*

American Methodism, Abingdon 1964, Vol. II, p. 610.

15. Luke Tyerman, *Praying William.* Cf. *Love and Life: the Story of J. Denholm Brash* by his Son, 'The Locked Study and the Open Heart', London 1913.

11 The Family

1. John Walsh in Davies and Rupp (eds), *A History of the Methodist Church in Great Britain*,Vol. I, p. 311.
2. Coley, *Life of Thomas Collins*, p. 99.
3. *Methodist Hymn Book*, 1933, No. 545. James Jones would be familiar with a conflation of this hymn and what from 1876 has been sung as 'Christ whose glory fills the skies'.
4. It is interesting to compare this record with that of W. R. Inge, the Dean of St Paul's almost a century later, who in the chapter 'Bereavement' in *Personal Religion and the Life of Devotion*, Longmans 1924, tells the story of his little girl, Paula, who died in 1923. Allow for the vast difference of culture between the two homes and the contrast between evangelical sentimentality and Anglican Platonist restraint, and the two lives have more in common than either has with a modern pagan or Methodist child.
5. Nicholas Bownde, *The True Doctrine of the Sabbath before and under the Law and in the time of the Gospel*, enlarged edition 1604. See Patrick Collinson, 'The Beginnings of English Sabbatarianism' in C. W. Dugmore and Charles Duggan (eds), *Studies in Church History*, Vol. I, Nelson 1964, pp. 207–21.

12 A Piety Based on Preaching

1. Cf. Erik Routley, *English Religious Dissent*, CUP 1960, pp. 168 ff.
2. H. R. McAdoo, *The Structure of Caroline Moral Theology*, Longmans 1948, p. 12 and elsewhere. 'The general medium of Anglican moral theology will be the sermon.'
3. A. Raymond George, 'Private Devotion in the Methodist Tradition', *Studia Liturgica*, Vol. IV, September 1963, p. 233.

13 Cheerfulness Breaking In

1. John H. S. Kent, *The Age of Disunity*, Epworth Press 1966, p. 102.

2. Richard Green. quoted by Henry D. Rack in *The Future of John Wesley's Methodism*, Epworth Press 1965, pp. 37–38.
3. For an interesting paragraph and footnotes on Dallinger see Rack, op. cit., p. 33; also J. F. C. Dakin in *Methodist Magazine*, January 1966.

14 The Holiness Movement and Responses

1. In the account of the Holiness Movement and the Fellowship of the Kingdom which follows I am particularly indebted to Dr Ian Randall's as yet unpublished thesis on 'The Holiness Movement in Methodism'.

15 The Liberal Reaction

1. R. N. Flew, *The Idea of Christian Perfection in Christian Theology*, OUP 1934, pp. 400–15.
2. W. B. Brash, *Love and Life*, Kelly 1913, ch. VI, 'The Sportsman'.
3. J. Alexander Findlay, *Jesus and His Parables*, Epworth Press 1950, p. 125.
4. John Ruskin, *Frondes Agrestes*.
5. T. R. and W. R. Maltby, *Studies in St Mark*, I, Manuals of Fellowship, Epworth Press 1920ff.
6. 'Of all the oddities about the parable of the sower, perhaps the strangest is this: there is still no agreement on what it was originally supposed to mean' (N. T. Wright, *Jesus and the Victory of God*, SPCK 1996, p. 230). For Wright's interpretation much influenced by the idea of the Kingdom see ibid., pp. 230–38. There is much less emphasis on the personality of Jesus, the lover of nature and of human souls.
7. A. L. Lilley, *Prayer in Christian Theology*, SCM Press 1924, p. 8.
8. R. N. Flew, *The Hymns of Charles Wesley*, Epworth Press 1953, pp. 69ff.
9. Kenneth Leech, *Soul Friend*, SPCK 1977.
10. Wakefield, *Robert Newton Flew*, p. 197: Cf. Lilley, *Prayer in Christian Theology*, p. 8.

16 The Groups

1. Ian Randall, 'Quest, Crusade and Fellowship', Fellowship of the Kingdom 1995 (extracted and adapted from his thesis on 'The Holiness Movement in Methodism').

2. J. A. Chapman, *The Supernatural Life*, Epworth Press 1934.

17 Catholics and Protestants

1. J. M. Turner, *Conflict and Reconciliation*, Epworth Press 1985, p. 181.
2. Henry Lunn, *The Secret of the Saints*, Heffer 1933, p. 5.
3. A. Kingsley Lloyd, quoted by T. S. Gregory in 'The Church which is His Body', Manual of Fellowship, Epworth Press 1933.
4. A. E. Whitham, *The Discipline and Culture of the Spiritual Life*, Hodder 1938. See the Introduction by Fiona Mary Whitham, p. 9.
5. Ibid., pp. 106–7.
6. Ibid.
7. Ibid.
8. Norman G. Dunning, *Samuel Chadwick*, London 1933, pp. 19–20.

18 Methodism and Protestantism

1. See Franz Hildebrandt, *From Luther to Wesley*, Lutterworth Press 1951.
2. Gordon Rupp, *Principalities and Powers*, Epworth Press 1952, *passim*.
3. W. F. Lofthouse in Davies and Rupp (eds), *A History of the Methodist Church in Great Britain*, Vol. I, p. 144.

19 Radical Spirituality

1. W. H. Auden, *Secondary Worlds*, Faber 1968, p. 139.

20 Methodism and the Vogue for Spirituality

1. Gordon S. Wakefield, *The Life of the Spirit in the World of Today*, Epworth Press 1969, pp. 139–59.
2. See, e.g., J. Neville Ward, *The Use of Praying*, Epworth Press 1967; *Five for Sorrow, Ten for Joy*, Epworth Press 1971; *Friday Afternoon*, Epworth Press 1971.

21 Restatements beyond Methodism

1. Dorothy Emmet, *Philosophers and Friends*, Macmillan 1996, pp. 22f.
2. *Hymns and Psalms*, No. 153. See Hildebrandt's fine exposition in *A Collection of Hymns*, pp. 11ff.
3. Donald Nicholl, *Holiness*, Darton, Longman and Todd 1981, p. 126.
4. Ibid., p. 38.
5. Ibid., p. 116.
6. Ibid., p. 146. The reference to the train journey to Auschwitz is my own.
7. See e.g. Murray Dell, *On a Huge Hill*, SCM Press 1998 and various writings of Maurice Wiles, e.g. *Faith and the Mystery of God*, SCM Press 1982, and 'Belief, Openness and Religious Commitment' in *Theology*, May/June 1998.

Index